Phoenician Hebrew Course
(Ancient and Paleo)

Free Live Online Ancient Phoenician Paleo Hebrew Course

Course offered monthly | 25 per class

To Enroll: zionlawschool.org/course-library

Requirement: 911 Ibaryath Rescue | Ancient Phoenician Paleo Hebrew International Edition

Ancient Phoenician Paleo Hebrew
International Edition

911 Ibaryath RESCUE

Jeremiah 8:8 How can you say, "We're wise, and the Law of The Most High is with us," when, in fact, the deceitful pen of the scribe has made it into something that deceives.

Uncover Scribal Errors & Outright Deception
Never Get Duped Again!
Authentic Pictograph Sounds

House of Yashar'al

Adults & Children
Beginners Level: Color Edition

Paleo-Ivriyt

Aleph Taw Aleph-Bet

- ✔ Free Notebook (56 Pages)
- ✔ Paleo-Hebrew Aleph-Bet
- ✔ Early, Middle & Late Scripts
- ✔ 67 Pictographs
- ✔ 23 Pictures

- ✔ 67 Handwriting Exercises
- ✔ Pronunciation
- ✔ Modern Hebrew Script
  - ✔ 22 Pictographs & 22 Handwriting Exercises
     Pronunciation

For Mother-Daughter Bonding Absolute Beginners Level

Learn Paleo-Hebrew Alef-Bet

- ✔ Free Notebook (56 Pages)
- ✔ Learn The Hebrew Alef-Bet
- ✔ Early, Middle & Late Scripts
- ✔ 67 Pictographs
- ✔ 23 Pictures

- ✔ 67 Handwriting Exercises
- ✔ Pronunciation

Color Edition

Hebrew Israelites

Copyright © 2019 Zion Law School

All rights reserved.

No part of this publication may be reproduced, distributed, or transmitted in any form or by any means, including photocopying, recording, information storage and retrieval systems, or other electronic or mechanical methods, without the prior written permission of the author, publisher or their lawful representative except in the case of brief quotations embodied in critical reviews and certain other noncommercial uses permitted by copyright law.

Independently published

Zion Law School
www.zionlawschool.org

Yachaana, Dr. Yasapa

Phoenician Hebrew 101

Biblical Hebrew
Ancient Phoenician Paleo Hebrew
Religion, Biblical Reference, Language Study, Bible

ISBN: 9781674915265

DEDICATION

This work is dedicated to the Most High and to everyone who has loyally supported me in filling my teaching assignment.

CONTENTS

Exodus 20:1-17 | Ten Commandments
1611 Authorized King James Version

Author's Note 9

Introduction 10

Exodus 20:1 17

Exodus 20:2 22

Exodus 20:3 28

Exodus 20:4 34

Exodus 20:5 41

Exodus 20:6 54

Exodus 20:7 59

Exodus 20:8 69

Exodus 20:9 72

Exodus 20:10 76

Exodus 20:11 87

Exodus 20:12 102

Exodus 20:13 112

Exodus 20:14 114

Exodus 20:15 116

Exodus 20:16 118

Exodus 20:17 121

ACKNOWLEDGMENTS

I want to say a special thank you to my dear friends and Zion Law School Scholars Lynette Hampton and Fredah Kaaria for encouraging me when I needed it and for consistently giving me great advice, and to Derek Hawker and Hadar Jones for consistently and gently reminding me to schedule the Ten Commandments Special Class that ultimately lead me to write this outstanding work, and to Sharah Burrell for the many heated conversations we shared that caused me to grow intellectually and increased my understanding of the Scriptures.

AUTHOR'S NOTE

In this language tool, I have made every effort to capture the basic Hebraic meaning, authentic pronunciation, and morphology of each Phoenician Hebrew word in the Ten Commandments recorded at Exodus 20:1-17 in the 1611 Authorized King James Version (AV) of the Bible. I use simple, easy to understand English to explain the grammar that the 1611 KJV (AV) translation team used in their rendering. A standardized gloss is provided next to each KJV rendering to demonstrate how words, phrases and sentences are constructed.

Strong's numbers are cited for each Phoenician Hebrew word. It is instructive to compare and contrast each Phoenician Hebrew word's Hebraic meaning to its rendering in the 1611 KJV and its gloss. Space is provided at the end of each verse for the reader to demonstrate his or her newly acquired knowledge by personally rendering each verse. Use any extra space to write your thoughts, feelings, findings and ideas. This is powerful, so do not skip it.

Because this work is based on a translation it is not free from the doctrines, traditions, political objectives, and theology of its translators. I do not address any of the above topics nor do I address cultural context or translation accuracy in this work. If you want to know more about these topics, visit us online at zionlawschool.org and enroll in the 503 Biblical Hebrew Translation Skills class and the 504 Ten Commandments class.

Dr. Yasapa
Dr. Yasapa, MD, MBA
Founder of Zion Law School

INTRODUCTION TO PHOENICIAN HEBREW GRAMMAR

In this chapter we will introduce you to the Biblical Phoenician Hebrew grammar, morphology, syntax (sentence structure) and concepts that the translators of the Authorized Version of the 1611 King James Bible applied in their rendering of Exodus 20:1-17 (the Ten Commandments).

Mastery of the concepts discussed in this chapter are critically important to understanding Phoenician Hebrew. Zion Law School wants to assist you on your path to learning our National Language. Our teaching methodology is fun, interactive, entertaining, and thorough. Zion Law School teaches pure Phoenician Hebrew only and we are the best Phoenician Hebrew school in the world. We offer a wide range of Phoenician Hebrew and English Language grammar courses. Visit us online at zionlawschool.org to check out our courses, diploma and certificate programs, and our unique Phoenician Hebrew products and services.

Phoenician Hebrew Nouns and Pronouns
Nouns are people, places, things, ideas and emotions. Here are some examples of nouns:

People: 𐤋𐤔𐤓𐤋 (Ya-Sha-Ra-La)

𐤄𐤓𐤔 (Sha-Ra-Ha)

𐤄𐤃𐤄 (Ha-Da-Ra)

Places: Zion, Jerusalem

Things: horse, table, land

Ideas or Emotions: wisdom, happiness, truth

Pronouns
Pronouns are words that take the place of nouns. Here are some pronouns:

I, you, he, she, them, and they

Adjectives
Phoenician Hebrew adjectives describe, modify and classify nouns (to add increased specificity to nouns). *Adjectives must agree in person, gender and number of the noun(s) they modify.*

Articles
In Phoenician Hebrew, there is a definite article ᗡ (the) but there is not an indefinite article ("a" chair, "an" apple). Consider Phoenician Hebrew nouns that occur without a definite article as indefinite. For example, the word 𐤌𐤉𐤄𐤋𐤀 (Ah-La-Ha-Ya-Ma) written without the definite article is rendered "𐤌𐤉𐤄𐤋𐤀" or "a 𐤌𐤉𐤄𐤋𐤀". Here is 𐤌𐤉𐤄𐤋𐤀 written with the definite article "𐤌𐤉𐤄𐤋𐤀ᗡ"—it is rendered "the 𐤌𐤉𐤄𐤋𐤀"

Conjunctions
Conjunctions are joining words. They join words, phrases and sentences together. The conjunction 𐤅 (Wa) never appears alone, rather it is always prefixed to another word. In Phoenician Hebrew, the conjunction 𐤅 performs the conjunction function. Here's are some examples that the conjunction 𐤅 takes:

𐤅 (Wa): and, but, even, also

Prepositions
Phoenician Hebrew prepositions describe relationships between words such as *under* the table, *over* the hump, *before* class, *during*

playtime, and other relationships not mentioned here. The table below shows some common prepositions.

Preposition	Meaning
𐤗𐤀 (Ah-Tha)	with, beside
𐤒𐤄𐤀 (Ah-Chaa-Ra)	behind, after
𐤋𐤀 (Ah-La)	to, toward
𐤋𐤉 (Ka-La)	All, each, every
𐤉 (Ka)	like, as, according to
𐤌𐤍 (Ma-Na)	from, out of
𐤌 (Ma)	from
𐤋𐤏 (O-La)	on, upon
𐤗𐤄𐤗 (Tha-Chaa-Tha)	under, below, instead of
𐤋 (La)	to, toward, for
𐤁 (Ba)	In, at, with, against, by

The word immediately after the preposition is called the *object of the preposition*.

The Definite Direct Object Marker

𐤗𐤀 (Ah-Tha) is the definite direct object marker. It is spelled exactly the same as the 𐤗𐤀, which is a preposition and is rendered "with" or "beside". Context will enable you to distinguish between the two forms.

The direct object is the word that receives the action of the verb.

In the sentence, "Fredah's arrow hit the bullseye", the object is "bullseye" because the bullseye was hit by the arrow. (That is to say, the bullseye received the action of the verb, "hit"). In the sentence above, bullseye is also the definite direct object because it has the definite article *the* bullseye. The definite direct object is never translated.

Phoenician Hebrew Verbs
Verbs are words that describe actions. They are sometimes called action words. Here are some examples of verbs:

Run, jump, build, shot

Subject
The subject of a sentence is a noun and is defined as the one who performs the action that the verb describes.

Object
The object of a sentence is defined as the receiver of the action that the verb describes.

Here is an example of how verbs, subjects and objects work together in a sentence:

Fredah shot an arrow that hit the bullseye.

The word that describes an action in the above sentence is "shot", so "shot" is the verb.

"Fredah" is the subject of the above sentence because "Fredah" shot the arrow. (Fredah performed the action of the verb).

The bullseye is the object of this sentence because the arrow hit the bullseye. (The bullseye received the action of the verb).

Verb Tenses
In Phoenician Hebrew, verbs either express a *completed action* or

an *incomplete action*. Here are examples of each:

Perfect Tense (Past): "Fredah shot an arrow" is a completed action because it already happened. The perfect tense is similar to the past tense in English.

Imperfect Tense (Future): "Fredah will shoot an arrow" is an incomplete action because it has not occurred yet. The imperfect tense is similar to the future tense in English. *Note: Modern Hebrew Grammarians combined the present and the future tenses to reflect the Greek custom of combining the present and future tenses.*

Imperfect Tense (Present): "Fredah is shooting an arrow" is an incomplete action because Fredah performs the action now. The imperfect tense is also similar to the present tense in English.

Carefully analyze the short list of perfect and imperfect verb conjugations below. Understanding this information is vital!

Perfect Tense	
Suffix	Meaning
א ת Ya-Tha-any root	I any root
ת Tha-any root	You any root
None-any root	He any root
ה Ha-any root	She any root

Imperfect Tense

Prefix	Conjugation	Literal Meaning	Translation
⟨Phoenician⟩ *Ah-Ha-Ya-Ha*	I will (1st Person)	I will be	I AM
⟨Phoenician⟩ *Tha-Ha-Ya-Ha*	you will (2nd Person)	you will be	you exist
⟨Phoenician⟩ *Ya-Ha-Ya-Ha* YHWH (YHVH)	he will (3rd Person Masculine)	he will be	he exists
⟨Phoenician⟩ *Tha-Ha-Ya-Ha*	she will (3rd Person Feminine)	she will be	she exists

What conclusions can you draw from your analysis each of the divine names (Ahayah and Yahuwah/Yahuah/YHWH (YHVH)) in the table above? Compare Strong's Numbers H3068, H1961, H1933 and H136.

Object of Verb Identifiers

⟨Phoenician⟩ Na-Ya-any word	me
⟨Phoenician⟩ Ka-any word	you
⟨Phoenician⟩ Wa-any word	him

Zion Law School offers Phoenician Hebrew and English grammar courses. Visit us online at www.zionlawschool.org to enroll or to get more of pure, rare, and unique Phoenician Hebrew products like you are presently enjoying.

The Construct State
When two nouns are next to each other they are said to be in the construct state and the word "of" must be inserted between them to render them in English.

Verb Stems
There are 7 verb stems in the Phoenician Hebrew Language. Each verb form expresses an action and voice that adds an additional nuance of meaning a word. Visit us online at www.zionlawschool.org if you would like to learn more about these verb forms or to enroll in a Phoenician Hebrew or English grammar course.

Volitional Verb Forms
The volitional verb forms are Imperative, Infinitive and Cohortative. They express a command, wish or desire. Imperative Verbs express a direct command such as "[you] go!" Imperative Verbs do not express a tense (perfect or imperfect) or the object of the sentence. They identify the action of the verb in addition to the gender (masculine or feminine) and number (singular or plural) of the subject of the sentence. (Note the exclamation point which makes Imperative Verbs easy to identify). Infinitive Verbs express an action such as "move". Infinitive Verbs do not express the tense (perfect of imperfect), subject or object of a sentence.

The Participle
In general, participles express actions that are happening now like "reading".

Exodus 20:1

| 𐤅𐤉𐤃𐤁𐤓 . 𐤀𐤋𐤄𐤉𐤌 . 𐤀𐤕 . 𐤊𐤋-𐤄𐤃𐤁𐤓𐤉𐤌 . 𐤄𐤀𐤋𐤄 . 𐤋𐤀𐤌𐤓 |
(saying)   (the these)   (words)   (all)   (God)   (and spake)

And God spake all these words, saying,

Phoenician Hebrew Word: 𐤅𐤉𐤃𐤁𐤓
Transliteration: Wa-Ya-Da-Ba-Ra
1611 KJV (AV) | Gloss: and spake | and-he-spake

Root Word: 𐤃𐤁𐤓 (verb) means to arrange, to speak, to subdue and is indexed to Strong's #1696. Brown-Driver-Brigg's Meanings: to speak, declare, converse, command, promise, warn, threaten, sing.

Prefix: 𐤉 (Ya) tells us that the verb 𐤃𐤁𐤓 is written in the imperfect tense, therefore, 𐤉𐤃𐤁𐤓 means "will speak". 𐤉 also tells us that the subject of 𐤃𐤁𐤓 is the 3rd person, masculine, singular, pronoun "he", thus 𐤉𐤃𐤁𐤓 means "he will speak".

𐤅 (Wa) is the conjunction "and". 𐤅 also functions to reverse the tense of a verb to which it is attached. Here, 𐤅 changes 𐤉𐤃𐤁𐤓 to the perfect tense, thus 𐤅𐤉𐤃𐤁𐤓 (Wa-Ya-Da-Ba-Ra) means "and he spake", "and he spoke". (It is instructive to note that 𐤅𐤉𐤃𐤁𐤓 is written in a verb form that expresses an intensive or intentional action).

Phoenician Hebrew Word: 𐤀𐤋𐤄𐤉𐤌
Transliteration: Ah-La-Ha-Ya-Ma
1611 KJV (AV) | Gloss: God | God

Base Word: 𐤀𐤋𐤅𐤄 (Ah-La-Wa-Ha) (Masculine, noun) (also spelled 𐤀𐤋𐤄) means a deity or the Deity and is indexed to

Strong's #433. Brown-Driver-Brigg's Meanings: 1) God, 2) false god. ᵃᵗˡᵃ is derived from ˡᵃ, which means strength. Adjectivally, ˡᵃ is used for a deity(s) or the Almighty. ˡᵃ was the most commonly used general designation for "deity" in the ancient Near East (see Strong's #410). ᵃᵗˡᵃ is a divine name in the Book of Job. It corresponds to the Aramaic "elahh" (see Strong's #426).

ᵃᵗˡᵃ (Ah-La-Wa-Ha) is believed to be a singular form of ʸᵛᵃˡᵃ (Ah-La-Ha-Ya-Ma) (plural, noun), which means gods, goddess, the supreme God, and magistrates, rulers, judges, divine ones, ones, angels. Brown-Driver-Brigg's Meanings: rulers, judges, divine ones, angels, gods, god, goddess, godlike one, works or special possessions of God, the (*true*) God, God.

Suffix: ʸᵛ (Ya-Ma) tells us that the gender of ᵃᵗˡᵃ is masculine and its number is plural.

Explanation: In Phoenician Hebrew, the subject is written after the verb. Because ʸᵛᵃˡᵃ (Ah-La-Ha-Ya-Ma) occurs after the verb ⁱᵈᵛᵗ ("and he spake"), ʸᵛᵃˡᵃ is the subject of the verb (the "*he*" in "and *he* spake"). ʸᵛᵃˡᵃ is singular because the "he" in "and God spake" is singular. This explains why the 1611 KJV replaced the "he" with "God" in its rendering, "and God spake".

Phoenician Hebrew Word: ˣᵃ
Transliteration: Ah-Tha
1611 KJV (AV) | Gloss: untranslated

Word: ˣᵃ (untranslated, particle, direct object pointer) is indexed at Strong's #853 and always written before the definite direct object of the last verb. Brown-Driver-Brigg's Meanings: sign of the definite direct object, not translated in English but generally preceding and indicating the accusative.

Explanation: Phoenician Hebrew verbs have both a subject and an object. Recall that the last verb in this verse was the word 𐤅𐤉𐤃𐤁𐤓 (Wa-Ya-Da-Ba-Ra) ("and God spake"). The root word 𐤃𐤁𐤓 is the "*spake*" in "and God *spake*". The subject of 𐤅𐤉𐤃𐤁𐤓 is the "he" in "and he spoke". Keep reading if you want to know what is the definite direct object of 𐤅𐤉𐤃𐤁𐤓.

A definite direct object may occur as a single word or phrase, and is always the written after the particle 𐤀𐤕. In other words, 𐤀𐤕 is always written before the definite direct object, which is why 𐤀𐤕 is called the "definite direct object pointer". The definite direct object of 𐤅𐤉𐤃𐤁𐤓 (Wa-Ya-Da-Ba-Ra) are the words 𐤄𐤊𐤋𐤄 and 𐤄𐤃𐤁𐤓𐤉𐤌 that occur one word after 𐤀𐤕. The 1611 KJV (AV) translators combined the words 𐤄𐤊𐤋𐤄 and 𐤄𐤃𐤁𐤓𐤉𐤌 to rendered them as the phrase— "all these words".

Phoenician Hebrew Word: 𐤊𐤋
Transliteration: Ka-La
1611 KJV (AV) | Gloss: all | all-of

Word: 𐤊𐤋 (masculine, singular, noun) means "any, all, complete, every" and is indexed to Strong's #3605. Brown-Driver-Brigg's Meanings: all, the whole, the whole of, any, each, every, anything, totality, everything.

Phoenician Hebrew Word: 𐤄𐤃𐤁𐤓𐤉𐤌
Transliteration: Ha-Da-Ba-Ra-Ya-Ma
1611 KJV (AV) | Gloss: words | the-things

Base Word: 𐤓𐤁𐤃 (Da-Ba-Ra) (masculine, plural, noun) means "words" and is indexed to Strong's #1697. Brown-Driver-Brigg's Meanings: speech, word, speaking, thing, saying, utterance, business, occupation, acts, matter, case, something. Prefix(es): Ha is an article that means "the".

Suffix(es): 𐤌𐤉 (Ya-Ma) tells us that this noun is plural.

Phoenician Hebrew Word: 𐤄𐤀𐤋𐤄
Transliteration: Ha-Ah-La-Ha
1611 KJV (AV) | Gloss: the these | the-these

Base Word: 𐤄𐤋𐤀 (Ah-La-Ha) (demonstrative, pronoun) means "these" and is indexed to Strong's #428.

Prefix(es): 𐤄 (Ha) is the article "the".

Explanation: The 1611 KJV translators combined the words 𐤄𐤋𐤀 and 𐤄𐤃𐤁𐤓𐤌 and rendered them as the phrase—"all these words". This phrase receives the action of the last verb which was 𐤃𐤁𐤓 ("spake"), therefore, the phrase 𐤄𐤋𐤀 * 𐤄𐤃𐤁𐤓𐤌 ("all these words") is the direct object of the verb 𐤃𐤁𐤓. Consequently, 𐤀𐤕 points to the phrase 𐤄𐤋𐤀 * 𐤄𐤃𐤁𐤓𐤌.

Phoenician Hebrew Word: 𐤋𐤀𐤌𐤓
Transliteration: La-Ah-Ma-Ra
1611 KJV (AV) | Gloss: saying | to-say

Root Word: 𐤀𐤌𐤓 (verb) (Ah-Ma-Ra) means "to say, speak, utter" and is indexed at Strong's #559. 𐤋𐤀𐤌𐤓 (La-Ah-Ma-Ra) expresses a simple action in the active voice and functions as a verbal noun.

Prefix(es): 𐤋 (La) is a preposition meaning "to" as in "to say".

It is your prerogative to translate this as "to say" or "saying". Write your own literal translation of Exodus 20:1 in the space below:

Ancient Script: _____
_____
_____
_____
_____

Paleo Script: _____
_____
_____
_____
_____
_____
_____

Exodus 20:2

𐤀𐤍𐤊𐤉 · 𐤉𐤄𐤅𐤄 · 𐤀𐤋𐤄𐤉 · 𐤀𐤔𐤓 · 𐤄𐤅𐤑𐤀𐤕𐤉 · 𐤌𐤀𐤓𐤑 ·
I   Lord, YHWH   thy God   which   haue brought thee   out of the land

| 𐤌𐤑𐤓𐤉𐤌 · 𐤌𐤁𐤉𐤕 · 𐤏𐤁𐤃𐤉𐤌
of Egypt   out of the house   of bondage

I am the Lord thy God, which haue brought thee out of the land of Egypt, out of the house of bondage:

Phoenician Hebrew Word: 𐤀𐤍𐤊𐤉
Transliteration: Ah-Na-Ka-Ya
1611 KJV (AV) | Gloss: I | I

Word: 𐤀𐤍𐤊𐤉 (pronoun, first person, singular) means "I" and is indexed to Strong's #595.

Phoenician Hebrew Word: 𐤉𐤄𐤅𐤄
Transliteration: Ya-Ha-Wa-Ha
1611 KJV (AV) | Gloss: Lord | Yahweh [YHWH (YHVH)]

Root Word: 𐤄𐤅𐤄 (Ha-Wa-Ha) (verb) means "to fall out, come to pass, become, be" and is indexed to Strong's #1961. Brown-Driver-Brigg's Meanings: to be, become, come to pass, exist, happen, fall out, [verb form nuances:] to happen, fall out, occur, take place, come about, come to pass, to come about, come to pass, to come into being, become, to arise, appear, come, to become, to become, to become like, to be instituted, be established, to be, to exist, be in existence, to abide, remain, continue (*with word of place or time*), to stand, lie, be in, be at, be situated (*with word of locality*), to accompany, be with, to occur, come to pass, be done, be brought about, to be done, be finished, be gone.

Prefix: 𐤉 (Ya) tells us that the subject of the verb 𐤄𐤅𐤄 (Ha-Wa-Ha) is the 3rd person, masculine, singular, pronoun "he", thus 𐤉𐤄𐤅𐤄 means "he exists" or any of the various meanings given above. Of course, context is always helpful to determine a word's meaning and how to render it in English. **Explanation**: Jewish people have a tradition of saying "adonai" (Strong's #136) when they read the name אהוה (YHWH (YHVH)). The Modern Hebrew vowel pointings in אהוה come from the vowel pointings in the word "adonai". The vowels are based on Jewish traditions and have nothing to do with the original pronunciation of אהוה.

Following the Greek custom, Jewish grammarians combined the present and future tenses of the ancient Phoenician Hebrew Language into one tense (the Imperfect tense). For example, the words Ahayah and YHWH (YHVH) are merely different tenses of the same verb, "hayah" (Strong's #1961). What are the present and future tense conjugations of the verb hayah and what are there meanings? Why is YHWH (YHVH) considered a divine name? There is much more to this topic! Do you want to know more? If yes, Zion Law School will teach you all there is to know, grammatically, about the divines. Visit us online at zionlawschool.org and enroll in the 503 Biblical Hebrew Translations Skills class and the 504 Ten Commandments class. We are looking forward to seeing you in class!

Phoenician Hebrew Word: אהיכם
Transliteration: Ah-La-Ha-Ya-Ka
1611 KJV (AV) | Gloss: thy God | God-of-you
Base Word: אלוה (Ah-La-Wa-Ha) (noun) (shortened spelling אלה) means a deity, or the Deity and is indexed to Strong's #433. אלוה is perhaps the singular form of אלהים (Ah-La-Ha-Ya-Ma) (Strong's #430) and means "gods in the ordinary sense; [plural or with the article] the supreme God; [plural refers to:] human or divine rulers, judges, magistrates, representatives at sacred places or as reflecting

divine majesty or power, super human beings such as God and angels; the sons of God or the sons of god = angels; god, goddess".

אלא is a Hebrew name for "God" that corresponds to the Aramaic elahh (Strong's #426). The origin of the term is unknown. אלא is a divine name in the Book of Job but it is rarely used as such in other Bible books. Brown-Driver-Brigg's: rulers, judges, divine ones, angels, gods, god, goddess, godlike one, works or special possessions of God, the (*true*) God, God.

Suffix(es): ימ (Ya-Ma) tells us that the gender of אלא (shortened spelling of אולא) is masculine and its number is plural.

י (Ka) is the 2nd person, masculine, singular possessive pronoun "[of] you", "your".
Explanation: Here is how this word is constructed:

Step 1: Base word אלא (Ah-La-Ha) (noun) + plural suffix ימ (Ya-Ma) + suffix י (Ka) (2nd person, masculine, singular possessive pronoun)

Step 2: Because יםאלא is a plural noun that is in the construct state, the י in ימ (Ya-Ma) must be deleted as shown here י + ~~מ~~ ימ + אלא which leaves י + ימ + אלא (Ah-La-Ha-Ya-Ka) to form the word יםאלא.

Context always determines if the noun יםאלא (Ah-La-Ha-Ya-Ka) (noun) is singular or plural. יםאלא describes אוהי (YHWH (YHVH)) which is singular, therefore, the noun ילהאך (Ah-La-Ha-Ya-Ka) is also singular.

Phoenician Hebrew Word: אשר
Transliteration: Ah-Sha-Ra
1611 KJV (AV) | Gloss: which | who

Word: אשר (Ah-Sha-Ra) (genderless, numberless, relative participle) means "who, what, which, that" and is indexed to Strong's #834. Brown-Driver-Brigg's Meanings: (relative participle) which, who, that which, (conjunction) that (in object clause), when, since, as, conditional if.

Phoenician Hebrew Word: הציאתיך
Transliteration: Ha-Wa-Taza-Ah-Tha-Ya-Ka
1611 KJV (AV) | Gloss: have brought thee | I-brought-out-you

Root word: יצא (Ya-Taza-Ah) (verb) means "to go out, come out, exit, go forth" (Brown-Driver-Brigg's) and is indexed to Strong's #3318.

Prefix(es): ה (Ha) tells us that this verb is a Form 6 verb, so it expresses causation – "make go out"

Suffix(es): תי (Tha-Ya) tells us that the subject of this verb is 1st person, singular and its tense is imperfect therefore we can render it – "I will make go out". ך (Ka) tells us that the object of this verb is 2nd person, masculine, singular – "I will make you go out".

Explanation: When a root word has י (Ya) in the first position and there is a prefix to the right of the י as is the case with this verb, the י must be changed to ו (Wa).

Phoenician Hebrew Word: ואמר

Transliteration: Ma-Ah-Ra-Taza
1611 KJV (AV) | Gloss: out of the land | from-land-of

Base Word: ⟨ᚺ⟩ (Ah-Ra-Taza) (masculine, noun) means "land", "country", "ground", "soil" and is indexed to Strong's #776. means "land" (masculine, noun) and is indexed to Strong's #776. Brown-Driver-Brigg's Meanings: land, whole earth (as opposed to a part), earth (inhabitants), land, country, territory, district, region, tribal territory, piece of ground, land of Canaan, Israel, inhabitants of land, Sheol, land without return, (*under*) world.

Prefix(es): ⟨⟩ (Ma) is a preposition that means "from".

Phoenician Hebrew Word: ⟨⟩
Transliteration: Ma-Taza-Ra-Ya-Ma
1611 KJV (AV) | Gloss: of Egypt | Egypt

Base Word: ⟨⟩ (Ma-Taza-Ra-Ya-Ma) is often rendered "Egyptians or double straits" (Brown-Driver-Brigg's) and is indexed to Strong's #4714. It is derived from the word ⟨⟩ (Ma-Taza-Ra) (noun), which means "straight".

Suffix(es): ⟨⟩ (Ya-Ma) in this case is dual in plurality, therefore, ⟨⟩ (Ma-Taza-Ra-Ya-Ma) means "two straits".

Explanation: Because ⟨⟩ (Ma-Ah-Ra-Taza) and ⟨⟩ (Ma-Taza-Ra-Ya-Ma) are both nouns and they are next to each other, they are in the Construct State. Therefore, you must insert "of" between them which renders the meaning as "from the land of two straits (mitsrayim)".

Phoenician Hebrew Word: ⟨⟩
Transliteration: Ma-Ba-Ya-Tha
1611 KJV (AV) | Gloss: out of the house | from-house-of

Base Word: ×𝟐𝟑 (Ba-Ya-Tha) (masculine, noun) means "a house", "family", "nation", "territory", "house, dwelling, habitation, shelter or abode of animals, human bodies (figuratively), of Sheol, of abode, of light and darkness, of land of Ephraim" (Brown-Driver-Brigg's) and is indexed to Strong's #1004.

Prefix(es): 𝒴 (Ma) is a preposition that means "from"

Phoenician Hebrew Word: 𝒴𝟐◁𝟑O
Transliteration: I-Ba-Da-Ya-Ma
1611 KJV (AV) | Gloss: of bondage | slavery

Base Word: ◁𝟑O (I-Ba-Da) (masculine, noun) means "servant" and is indexed to Strong's #5650. Brown-Driver-Brigg's Meanings: slave, servant, slave, servant, man-servant, subjects, servants, worshippers (of God), servant (in a special sense as prophets, Levites etc), servant (of Israel), servant (as form of address between equals).

Suffix(es): 𝒴𝟐 (Ya-Ma) tells us that ◁𝟑O is written in the plural, thus it is rendered—"servants" or "bondage".

Explanation: ×𝟐𝟑𝒴 (Ma-Ba-Ya-Tha) and 𝒴𝟐◁𝟑O (I-Ba-Da-Ya-Ma) are both nouns. When two nouns are next to each other they are in the construct state, therefore, we must insert the word "of" between them, which in this case yields—"from the house of servants" or "from the house of bondage".

Write your own literal translation of Exodus 20:2 in the space below:

Ancient Script: _____
_____
_____
_____

Paleo Script:

Exodus 20:3

𐤋𐤏𐤉-𐤋𐤏· 𐤉𐤇𐤀𐤌· 𐤉𐤋𐤀𐤋𐤄· 𐤉𐤋-𐤄𐤉𐤄𐤉 ·𐤀𐤋
　me　 before　　other　　　Gods　　　you shalt haue　　No

Thou shalt haue no other Gods before me.

Phoenician Hebrew Word: 𐤀𐤋
Transliteration: La-Ah
1611 KJV (AV) | Gloss: No | not

Word: 𐤀𐤋 (negative participle) is indexed to Strong's #3808 and means "not". Brown-Driver-Brigg's Meanings: not, no, not (with verb — absolute prohibition), not (with modifier — negation), nothing (substantive), without (with particle), before (of time).

Explanation: 𐤀𐤋 negates the action of the verb that comes immediately after it. Stated another way, 𐤀𐤋 negates the action of the verb it is associated with.

Phoenician Hebrew Word: 𐤄𐤉𐤄𐤉
Transliteration: Ya-Ha-Ya-Ha
1611 KJV (AV) | Gloss: shall have | he shall be

Root Word: 𐤄𐤉𐤄 (Ha-Ya-Ha) (verb) is indexed to Strong's #1961 and means "to be, become, come to pass, exist, happen, fall out" (Brown-Driver-Brigg's).

Prefix(es): 𐤉 (Ya) tells us that this verb is in the imperfect tense and the subject of this verb is the 3rd person, masculine, singular pronoun "he will exist".

Explanation: This verb's (𐤄𐤉𐤄) action is negated because the negative participle 𐤀𐤋 (La-Ah) is written just before 𐤄𐤉𐤄. Therefore, is rendered—"he will not exist".

Phoenician Hebrew Word: 𐤊𐤋
Transliteration: La-Ka
1611 KJV (AV) | Gloss: you | to you

Word: 𐤊𐤋 is constructed from a prefix and a suffix only.

Prefix(es): 𐤋 (La) is the preposition "for".

Suffix: 𐤊 (Ka) is the 2nd person, masculine, singular a pronoun "you".

Phoenician Hebrew Word: 𐤌𐤉𐤄𐤋𐤀
Transliteration: Ah-La-Ha-Ya-Ma
1611 KJV (AV) | Gloss: gods | gods

Base Word: 𐤄𐤅𐤋𐤀 (Ah-La-Wa-Ha) (perhaps a singular form of 𐤌𐤉𐤄𐤋𐤀, noun) means "god" and is indexed to Strong's #433. 𐤄𐤅𐤋𐤀 is a Hebrew name for "God" that corresponds to the Aramaic elahh (Strong's #426)". 𐤄𐤅𐤋𐤀 is a divine name in the Book of Job but it is rarely used as such in other Bible books. Brown-Driver-Brigg's Meanings: rulers, judges, divine ones, angels, gods, god, goddess, godlike one, works or special possessions of God, the (true) God, God.

Suffix: 𐤌𐤉 (Ya-Ma) tells us that the noun 𐤄𐤅𐤋𐤀 is masculine and plural.

Explanation: 𐤌𐤉𐤄𐤋𐤀 (Ah-La-Ha-Ya-Ma) occurs after the verb 𐤉𐤄𐤉𐤄 ("he will exist"), therefore, 𐤌𐤉𐤄𐤋𐤀 is the subject of the verb 𐤉𐤄𐤉𐤄. (In Phoenician Hebrew Language, the verb occurs before the subject). In other words, 𐤌𐤉𐤄𐤋𐤀 is the "he" in "he will exist". Furthermore, the "he" is singular therefore 𐤌𐤉𐤄𐤋𐤀 is singular.

Phoenician Hebrew Word: 𐤌𐤉𐤓𐤇𐤀
Transliteration: Ah-Chaa- Ra-Ya-Ma
1611 KJV (AV) | Gloss: other | other

Base Word: 𐤓𐤇𐤀 (Ah-Chaa-Ra) (adjective) is indexed to Strong's #312 and means "hinder, next, other, another". Brown-Driver-Brigg's Meanings: are "another, other, following, following, further, other, different".

Suffix: 𐤌𐤉 (Ya-Ma) tells us that this adjective is masculine, plural.

Explanation: This adjective, 𐤌𐤉𐤓𐤇𐤀 (Ah-Chaa- Ra-Ya-Ma), describes the word that occurred immediately before it (𐤌𐤉𐤋𐤀). Phoenician Hebrew adjectives must agree in gender and number with the nouns they describe. 𐤌𐤉𐤋𐤀 (gods) is plural, therefore, 𐤌𐤉𐤓𐤇𐤀 (other) has to be plural. The translators combine the words 𐤌𐤉𐤓𐤇𐤀 and 𐤌𐤉𐤋𐤀 to form the phrase 𐤌𐤉𐤓𐤇𐤀 * 𐤌𐤉𐤋𐤀, which is the object of the verb 𐤄𐤉𐤄 ("exists"). The subject of 𐤄𐤉𐤄 is masculine, singular. So, what is the best way to render this phrase? Read on if you want to know!

The direct object must agree in number with its verb. Because the "he" in the verb 𐤉𐤄𐤉𐤄 ("he will exist") is singular, the direct object 𐤌𐤉𐤓𐤇𐤀 * 𐤌𐤉𐤋𐤀 (phrase) must also be singular in order to agree with its verb. Here is an example rendering of this phrase—"other mighty one", "another mighty one", other powerful energy", "other supreme judge", "another supreme ruler", and "another powerful one".

At Zion Law School, we thoroughly cover all topics presented in this work. To learn more, visit us online at zionlawschool.org and enroll in the Free Live Online Ancient Phoenician Paleo

Hebrew Course, 503 Biblical Hebrew Translations Skill and 504 Ten Commandments or to get more unique and rare Phoenician Hebrew products and services.

Phoenician Hebrew Word: ᛚ O
Transliteration: I-La
1611 KJV (AV) | Gloss: before | before

Word: ᛚ O (I-La) is a preposition indexed to Strong's #5921 and means "upon". Brown-Driver-Brigg's Meanings: "upon, on the ground of, according to, on account of, on behalf of, concerning, beside, in addition to, together with, beyond, above, over, by, on to, towards, to, against (preposition), down upon, upon, on, from, up upon, up to, towards, over towards, to, against (with verbs of motion).

Phoenician Hebrew Word: ᛚ ᛡ ᛡ
Transliteration: Pa-Na-Ya
1611 KJV (AV) | Gloss: me | presence-of-me

Base Word: ᛚ ᛡ ᛡ (Pa-Na-Ya) (noun) is indexed to Strong's #6437 and means to turn, by implication to face, appear, look, etc. ᛚ ᛡ ᛡ is always written in the plural form by adding the plural suffix ᛡ ᛚ (Ya-Ma). Brown-Driver-Brigg's Meanings: face, face, faces, presence, person, face (of seraphim or cherubim), face (of animals), face, surface (of ground).

Suffix: ᛚ (Ya) is the 1st, singular, possessive pronoun "my" or "of me"

Explanation: Translators combine the words ᛚ O (I-La) and ᛚ ᛡ ᛡ (Pa-Na-Ya) which creates the phrase, ᛚ O * ᛚ ᛡ ᛡ ("gods before me", "in my presence", "in my face", etc.).

Here's how the word ᛚ ᛡ ᛡ (noun) is constructed:

Step 1: The root word 𐤋𐤍𐤐 (noun) + the plural suffix 𐤌𐤉 (Ya-Ma) + possessive pronoun 𐤉 (Ya) forms 𐤉𐤌𐤉𐤄𐤍𐤐 (Pa-Na-Ha-Ya-Ma-Ya).

Step 2: The 𐤄 must be deleted as shown here (𐤉𐤌𐤉~~𐤄~~𐤍𐤐) due to the presence of plural suffix, 𐤌𐤉, which leaves 𐤍𐤐 (Pa-Na) + 𐤌𐤉 (Ya-Ma) + 𐤉 (Ya).

Step 3: Whenever a plural noun is in the construct state, the 𐤌 in 𐤌𐤉 must be deleted as shown here 𐤉~~𐤌~~𐤉𐤄𐤍𐤐, which leaves 𐤍𐤐 + 𐤉 + 𐤉.

Step 4: Any double pictographs such as 𐤉 and 𐤉 must be reduced to a single pictograph, which yields 𐤍𐤐 + 𐤉 and forms the word 𐤉𐤍𐤐 (Pa-Na-Ya).

Write your own literal translation of Exodus 20:3 in the space below:

Ancient Script: _____
_____
_____
_____

Paleo Script: _____
_____
_____
_____

Exodus 20:4

𐤀𐤋 · 𐤅𐤔𐤏𐤄 𐤋𐤊 · 𐤐𐤎𐤋 · 𐤊𐤋 𐤕𐤌𐤅𐤍𐤄 𐤅𐤊𐤋 𐤀𐤔𐤓 ·
  Not   thou shalt make unto thee graven image or any likenesse that is

𐤁𐤔𐤌𐤉𐤌 · 𐤌𐤌𐤏𐤋 · 𐤅𐤀𐤔𐤓 · 𐤁𐤀𐤓𐤑 · 𐤌𐤕𐤇𐤕 · 𐤅𐤀𐤔𐤓 ·
  in heauen aboue or that is in the earth beneath or that is

𐤁𐤌𐤉𐤌 · 𐤌𐤕𐤇𐤕 · 𐤋𐤀𐤓𐤑 ·
  in the water vnder the earth

Thou shalt not make vnto thee any grauen Image, or any likenesse of any thing that is in heauen aboue, or that is in the earth beneath, or that is in the water vnder the earth.

Phoenician Hebrew Word: 𐤀𐤋
Transliteration: La-Ah
1611 KJV (AV) | Gloss: not | not

Word: 𐤀𐤋 (negative participle) is indexed to Strong's #3808 and means "not". Brown-Driver-Brigg's Meanings: not, no, not (*with verb — absolute prohibition*), not (*with modifier — negation*), nothing (*substantive*), without (*with particle*), before (*of time*).

Explanation: 𐤀𐤋 negates the action of the verb that comes immediately after it. Stated another way, 𐤀𐤋 negates the action of the verb it is associated with.

Phoenician Hebrew Word: 𐤕𐤏𐤔𐤄
Transliteration: Tha-I-Sha-Ha
1611 KJV (AV) | Gloss: thou shalt make | you-shall-make

Root Word: 𐤏𐤔𐤄 (I-Sha-Ha) (verb) means "do", "make" and is indexed to Strong's #6213. Brown-Driver-Brigg's Meanings: to do, fashion, accomplish, make, work, produce, to deal (*with*), to act, act with effect, effect, to make, to produce, to prepare, to make (*an offering*), to attend to, put in order, to observe, celebrate, to acquire (*property*), to appoint, ordain, institute, to bring about, to use, to spend, pass.

Prefix(es): 𐤕 (Tha) tells us that the verb 𐤏𐤔𐤄 is an incomplete action that will occur in the future. Thus, ᴀWOX (Tha-I-Sha-Ha) (verb) means "will do". X also tells us that the subject of ᴀWO is the 2nd person, masculine, singular pronoun "you". Therefore, ᴀWOX means—"you will do".

Explanation: "Do" and "make" are equivalent words. Context determines how to best render this word. Because the negative participle ᴀl (La-Ah) occurs before ᴀWOX, the action of the verb ᴀWO is negated—"you will not make".

Phoenician Hebrew Word: ᵞl
Transliteration: La-Ka
1611 KJV (AV) | Gloss: unto thee | for you
Word: No base word.

Prefix(es): l (La) is a preposition that means "for".

Suffix: ᵞ (Ka) is the 2nd person, masculine, singular pronoun "you".

Phoenician Hebrew Word: lꟻJ
Transliteration: Pa-Sa-La
1611 KJV (AV) | Gloss: graven image | carved-image

Word: lꟻJ (masculine, noun) is indexed to Strong's #6459 and means "an idol". Brown-Driver-Brigg's Meanings: idol, image.

Phoenician Hebrew Word: lᵞꓘ
Transliteration: Wa-Ka-La
1611 KJV (AV) | Gloss: or any | or-any-of

Base Word: lᵞ (masculine, singular, noun) means "any, all, complete, every" and is indexed to Strong's #3605. Brown-

Driver-Brigg's Meanings: all, the whole, the whole of, any, each, every, anything, totality, everything.

Prefix: 𐤅 (Wa) is the conjunction "and".

Explanation: Does the context suggest that "or" is a better translation than "and"? What is the relationship between "and" and "or"? How does the use of either word effect the meaning of this verse?

Phoenician Hebrew Word: 𐤀𐤔𐤓𐤍𐤄
Transliteration: Tha-Ma-Wa-Na-Ha
1611 KJV (AV) | Gloss: likeness | form

Word: 𐤀𐤔𐤓𐤍𐤄 (Tha-Ma-Wa-Na-Ha) (feminine noun) is indexed to Strong's #8544 and means "fashioned", "likeness", "image". Brown-Driver-Brigg's Meanings: form, image, likeness, representation, semblance.

Phoenician Hebrew Word: 𐤀𐤔𐤓
Transliteration: Ah-Sha-Ra
1611 KJV (AV) | Gloss: that is | that

Word: 𐤀𐤔𐤓 (Ah-Sha-Ra) (genderless, numberless, relative participle) means "who, what, which, that" and is indexed to Strong's #834. Brown-Driver-Brigg's Meanings: (relative participle) which, who, that which, (conjunction) that (in object clause), when, since, as, conditional if.

Phoenician Hebrew Word: 𐤁𐤔𐤌𐤉𐤌
Transliteration: Ba-Sha-Ma-Ya-Ma
1611 KJV (AV) | Gloss: in heaven | in-the-heaven

Base Word: 𐤔𐤌𐤉𐤌 (Sha-Ma-Ya-Ma) (masculine, noun) is indexed to Strong's #8064 and means "sky". Brown-Driver-Brigg's Meanings: heaven, heavens, sky, visible heavens, as abode of the stars, as the visible universe, the sky, atmosphere, etc., Heaven (as the abode of God).

Prefix(es): ߉ (Ba) is a preposition that means "in".

Phoenician Hebrew Word: ܐܘܥܠ
Transliteration: Ma-Ma-I-La
1611 KJV (AV) | Gloss: above | from-above

Base Word: ܥܠ (Ma-I-La) (adverb) indexed to Strong's #4605 and means "upward", "above", "overhead", "from the top". Brown-Driver-Brigg's Meanings: higher part, upper part (substantive), above (adverb), on the top of, above, on higher ground than (preposition), upwards, higher, above (with locative).

Prefix(es): ܡ (Ma) is the preposition "from".

Explanation: ܥܠ and the prefix ܡ are rendered "above".

Phoenician Hebrew Word: ܪܫܐܘ
Transliteration: Wa-Ah-Sha-Ra
1611 KJV (AV) | Gloss: or that is | or-that

Word: ܪܫܐ (Ah-Sha-Ra) (genderless, numberless, relative participle) means "who, what, which, that" and is indexed to Strong's #834. Brown-Driver-Brigg's Meanings: (relative participle) which, who, that which, (conjunction) that (in object clause), when, since, as, conditional if.

Prefix(es): ܘ (Wa) is a conjunction that means "and". Depending on the context, ܘ can be rendered "or". What problems do you see with this?

Phoenician Hebrew Word: ܒܐܪܨ
Transliteration: Ba-Ah-Ra-Taza

1611 KJV (AV) | Gloss: in the earth | in the earth

Base Word: ⟨ᴴ⟩ means "land" (masculine, noun) and is indexed to Strong's #776. Brown-Driver-Brigg's Meanings: land, whole earth (as opposed to a part), earth (inhabitants), country, territory, district, region, tribal territory, piece of ground, land of Canaan, Israel, inhabitants of land, Sheol, land without return, (under) world.

Prefix: ᵍ (Ba) is the preposition "in".

Phoenician Hebrew Word: ⟨XHXY⟩
Transliteration: Ma-Tha-Chaa-Tha
1611 KJV (AV) | Gloss: beneath | from-below

Base Word: ⟨XHX⟩ (Tha-Chaa-Tha) (noun) is indexed to Strong's #8478 and means "bottom (depressed)", "under", "below", "underneath". Brown-Driver-Brigg's Meanings: the under part, beneath, instead of, as, for, for the sake of, flat, unto, where, whereas, sweetness, subjection, woman, being burdened or oppressed (figuratively), of subjection or conquest, what is under one, in place of, instead of (in transferred sense), in place of, in exchange or return for (of things mutually interchanged), instead of, instead of that, in return for that, in, under, into the place of, from under, from beneath, from under the hand of, from his place, beneath.

Prefix: ᵞ (Ma) is the preposition "from".

Explanation: When the base word ⟨XHX⟩ (Tha-Chaa-Tha) and the prefix ᵞ (Ma) are written together (⟨XHX⟩ + ᵞ), they combine (⟨XHXY⟩) to mean—"below".

Phoenician Hebrew Word: ⟨ᐤW⟨⟩⟩
Transliteration: Wa-Ah-Sha-Ra
1611 KJV (AV) | Gloss: or that is | or that

Word: 𐤀𐤔𐤓 (Ah-Sha-Ra) (genderless, numberless, relative participle) means "who, what, which, that" and is indexed to Strong's #834. Brown-Driver-Brigg's Meanings: (relative participle) which, who, that which, (conjunction) that (in object clause), when, since, as, conditional if.

Phoenician Hebrew Word: 𐤌𐤉𐤌𐤁
Transliteration: Ba-Ma-Ya-Ma
1611 KJV (AV) | Gloss: in the water | in-the-water
Base Word: 𐤌𐤉𐤌 (Ma-Ya-Ma) (masculine, noun) indexed at Strong's #4325 and means water. Brown-Driver-Brigg's Meanings: water, waters, water of the feet, urine, of danger, violence, transitory things, refreshment (figuratively).
Prefix(es): 𐤁 (Ba) is the preposition "in".

Phoenician Hebrew Word: 𐤌𐤕𐤇𐤕
Transliteration: Ma-Tha-Chaa-Tha
1611 KJV (AV) | Gloss: under | from-under
Base Word: 𐤕𐤇𐤕 (Tha-Chaa-Tha) is indexed to Strong's #8478 and means "bottom (depressed)", "under", "below", "underneath". Brown-Driver-Brigg's Meanings: the under part, beneath, instead of, as, for, for the sake of, flat, unto, where, whereas, sweetness, subjection, woman, being burdened or oppressed (figuratively), of subjection or conquest, what is under one, in place of, instead of (in transferred sense), in place of, in exchange or return for (of things mutually interchanged), instead of, instead of that, in return for that, in, under, into the place of, from under, from beneath, from under the hand of, from his place, under, beneath.

Prefix(es): When the base word 𐤕𐤇𐤕 (Tha-Chaa-Tha) and the prefix 𐤌 (Ma) are written together (𐤕𐤇𐤕 + 𐤌), they combine

(𐤗𐤇𐤕𐤅) to mean—"below".

Phoenician Hebrew Word: 𐤋𐤀𐤓𐤑
Transliteration: La-Ah-Ra-Taza
1611 KJV (AV) | Gloss: in the earth | to-the-earth
Base Word: 𐤀𐤓𐤑 (Ah-Ra-Taza) (masculine, noun) means "land", "country", "ground", "soil" and is indexed to Strong's #776. means "land" (masculine, noun) and is indexed to Strong's #776. Brown-Driver-Brigg's Meanings: land, whole earth (as opposed to a part), earth (inhabitants), land, country, territory, district, region, tribal territory, piece of ground, land of Canaan, Israel, inhabitants of land, Sheol, land without return, (*under*) world.
Prefix(es): 𐤋 (La) is the preposition "to".

Write your own literal translation of Exodus 20:4 in the space below:

Ancient Script: _____
_____
_____
_____
_____

Paleo Script:_____
_____
_____
_____
_____

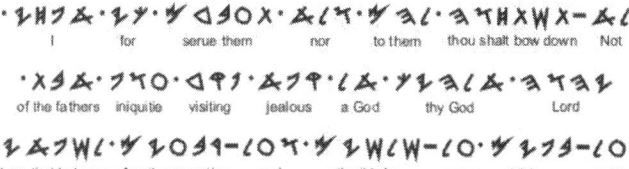

Thou shalt not bow downe thy selfe to them, nor serue them: For I the Lord thy God am a iealous God, visiting the iniquitie of the fathers vpon the children, vnto the thirde and fourth generation of them that hate me:

Phoenician Hebrew Word: ⟨⟩
Transliteration: La-Ah
1611 KJV (AV) | Gloss: not | not

Word: ⟨⟩ (negative participle) is indexed to Strong's #3808 and means "not". Brown-Driver-Brigg's Meanings: not, no, not (with verb — absolute prohibition), not (with modifier — negation), nothing (substantive), without (with particle), before (of time).

Explanation: ⟨⟩ negates the action of the verb that comes immediately after it. Stated another way, ⟨⟩ negates the action of the verb it is associated with.

Phoenician Hebrew Word: ⟨⟩
Transliteration: Tha-Sha-Tha-Chaa-Wa-Ha
1611 KJV (AV) | Gloss: Thou shalt bow down | you-shall-bow-down

Root Word: ⟨⟩ (Sha-Chaa-Ha) (verb) is indexed to Strong's #7812 and means "bow down". Brown-Driver-Brigg's Meanings: to bow down; [verb form nuances:] to depress (figuratively), to bow down, prostrate oneself, before superior in homage, before God in worship, before false gods, before angel.

Prefix: 𐤕 (Tha) tells us that 𐤄𐤅𐤇𐤕𐤔𐤕 (Tha-Sha-Tha-Chaa-Wa-Ha) (verb) is in the imperfect tense and the subject of 𐤄𐤅𐤇𐤕𐤔𐤕 is the 2nd person, masculine, singular, pronoun "you", thus 𐤄𐤅𐤇𐤕𐤔𐤕 means "you will bow down". Because 𐤄𐤅𐤇𐤕𐤔𐤕 is written in Verb Form 7, it means "you will bow thy selfe down", "you will bow yourself down".

Infix: The prefix 𐤄𐤕 (Ha-Tha) in a verb tells us that the verb is written in Verb Form 7. Notice that the prefix 𐤄𐤕 is not seen in the word 𐤄𐤅𐤇𐤕𐤔𐤕 whose root word is 𐤅𐤇𐤔 (verb). Actually, the prefix 𐤄𐤕 is present but in a modified form which we will call a unique spelling. In fact, there are two unique spellings involved in the construction of 𐤄𐤅𐤇𐤕𐤔𐤕 (Tha-Sha-Tha-Chaa-Wa-Ha).

Here's how the word 𐤄𐤅𐤇𐤕𐤔𐤕 (Tha-Sha-Tha-Chaa-Wa-Ha) is constructed:

Step 1: The prefix 𐤕 is added to the root word 𐤅𐤇𐤔 as shown here 𐤅𐤇𐤔 + 𐤕 which forms 𐤅𐤇𐤔𐤕.

Unique Spelling #1
Step 2: The prefix 𐤄𐤕 is added to 𐤅𐤇𐤔𐤕 as shown here: 𐤄𐤕 + 𐤅𐤇𐤔𐤕 which forms 𐤅𐤇𐤔𐤕𐤕𐤄

(The presence of the prefix 𐤄𐤕 attached to a verb indicates that the verb is written in Verb Form 7).

Step 3:
The 𐤄 in 𐤄𐤕 must be deleted as shown here: 𐤅𐤇𐤔𐤕𐤕𐤄̶ which leaves 𐤅𐤇𐤔𐤕𐤕

Step 4: The 𐤕 (remaining from the prefix 𐤕𐤄) is inserted into 𐤄𐤇𐤔𐤕𐤕 (step 3) between the 𐤇 (Chaa) and the 𐤔 (Sha) as shown here: 𐤄𐤇𐤕𐤔𐤕

Unique Spelling #2

Step 6: The 𐤅 (Wa) is inserted between the 𐤇 (Chaa) and the (Ha) as shown here: 𐤄𐤅𐤇𐤔𐤕 which completes the construction of the word 𐤄𐤅𐤇𐤔𐤕.

Explanation: The presence of the negative participle 𐤀𐤋 (La-Ah) before 𐤄𐤅𐤇𐤔𐤕 (Tha-Sha-Tha-Chaa-Wa-Ha) negates the action of 𐤄𐤅𐤇𐤔𐤕 and changes its meaning to "you will not bow yourself down".

Phoenician Hebrew Word: 𐤌𐤄𐤋
Transliteration: La-Ha-Ma
1611 KJV (AV) | Gloss: to them | to-them
Word: No base word. No Strong's number.

Prefix: 𐤋 (La) is the preposition "for".

Suffix: 𐤌𐤄 (Ha-Ma) is the 3rd person, masculine, plural, pronoun "them".

Phoenician Hebrew Word: 𐤀𐤋𐤅
Transliteration: Wa-Ah-La
1611 KJV (AV) | Gloss: nor | and-not

Word: 𐤀𐤋 (negative participle) means not and is indexed to Strong's #3808. Brown-Driver-Brigg's Meanings: not, no, not (with verb — absolute prohibition), not (with modifier — negation), nothing (substantive), without (with particle), before (of time).

Prefix: 𐤅 (Wa) is the conjunction "and".

Explanation: 𐤀𐤋 (negative participle) negates the action of the verb that comes immediately after it. In other words, 𐤀𐤋 negates the action of the verb it is associated with. In this case, 𐤀𐤋 negates the action of the next verb 𐤌𐤃𐤁𐤏𐤕 (Tha-I-Ba-Da-Ma) that occurs immediately after 𐤀𐤋.

Phoenician Hebrew Word: 𐤌𐤃𐤁𐤏𐤕
Transliteration: Tha-I-Ba-Da-Ma
1611 KJV (AV) | Gloss: serve them | you-shall-serve-them

Root Word: 𐤃𐤁𐤏 (I-Ba-Da) (verb) is indexed to Strong's #5647 and means serve. Brown-Driver-Brigg's Meanings: to work, serve; [verb form nuances]: to labour, work, do work, to work for another, serve another by labour, to serve as subjects, to serve (*God*), to serve (with Levitical service), to be worked, be tilled (of land), to make oneself a servant, to be worked, to compel to labour or work, cause to labour, cause to serve, to cause to serve as subjects, to be led or enticed to serve.

Prefix(es): 𐤕 (Tha) tells us that the tense of 𐤌𐤃𐤁𐤏𐤕 (Tha-I-Ba-Da-Ma) (verb) is imperfect. It also tells us that the subject of 𐤃𐤁𐤏 is the 2nd person, masculine, singular "you", thus 𐤃𐤁𐤏𐤕 means "you will serve".

Suffix: 𐤌 (Ma) tells us that the object of the verb, 𐤃𐤁𐤏𐤕 (Tha-I-Ba-Da), is the 3rd person, masculine plural pronoun "them", thus 𐤌𐤃𐤁𐤏𐤕 means "you will serve them".

Explanation: 𐤀𐤋 (La-Ah) (negative participle) negates the action of the last verb 𐤌𐤃𐤁𐤏𐤕 that is written immediately after it, thus "you will not serve them".

Phoenician Hebrew Word: 𐤊𐤉
Transliteration: Ka-Ya
1611 KJV (AV) | Gloss: for | for

Word: 𐤊𐤉 (conjunction) is indexed to Strong's #3588 and means "because". Brown-Driver-Brigg's Meanings: that, for, because, when, as though, as, because that, but, then, certainly, except, surely, since.

Phoenician Hebrew Word: 𐤀𐤍𐤊𐤉
Transliteration: Ah-Na-Ka-Ya
1611 KJV (AV) | Gloss: I | I

Word: 𐤀𐤍𐤊𐤉 is indexed to Strong's #595 and means "I". Brown-Driver-Brigg's Meanings: I (first person singular).

Phoenician Hebrew Word: 𐤉𐤄𐤅𐤄
Transliteration: Ya-Ha-Wa-Ha
1611 KJV (AV) | Gloss: Lord | Yahweh

Root Word: 𐤄𐤅𐤄 (Ha-Wa-Ha) (verb) means "to fall out, come to pass, become, be" and is indexed to Strong's #1961. Brown-Driver-Brigg's Meanings: to be, become, come to pass, exist, happen, fall out, [verb form nuances:] to happen, fall out, occur, take place, come about, come to pass, to come about, come to pass, to come into being, become, to arise, appear, come, to become, to become, to become like, to be instituted, be established, to be, to exist, be in existence, to abide, remain, continue (with word of place or time), to stand, lie, be in, be at, be situated (with word of locality), to accompany, be with, to occur, come to pass, be done, be brought about, to be done, be finished, be gone.

Prefix: 𐤉 (Ya) tells us that the subject of the verb 𐤄𐤅𐤄 (Ha-Wa-Ha) is the 3rd person, masculine, singular, pronoun "he", thus 𐤉𐤄𐤅𐤄 means "he exists" or any of the various meanings given above. Of course, context is always helpful to determine a word's meaning and how to render it in English. **Explanation**: Jewish people have a tradition of saying "adonai" (Strong's #136) when they read the name 𐤉𐤄𐤅𐤄 (YHWH (YHVH)). The Modern Hebrew vowel pointings in 𐤉𐤄𐤅𐤄 come from the vowel pointings in the word "adonai". The vowels are based on Jewish traditions and have nothing to do with the original pronunciation of 𐤉𐤄𐤅𐤄.

Following the Greek custom, Jewish grammarians combined the present and future tenses of the ancient Phoenician Hebrew Language into one tense (the Imperfect tense). For example, the words Ahayah and YHWH (YHVH) are merely different tenses of the same verb, "hayah" (Strong's #1961). What are the present and future tense conjugations of the verb hayah and what are there meanings? Why is YHWH (YHVH) considered a divine name? There is much more to this topic! Do you want to know more? If yes, Zion Law School will teach you all there is to know, grammatically, about the divines. Visit us online at zionlawschool.org and enroll in the 503 Biblical Hebrew Translations Skills class and the 504 Ten Commandments class. We are looking forward to seeing you in class!

Phoenician Hebrew Word: 𐤊𐤉𐤄𐤋𐤀
Transliteration: Ah-La-Ha-Ya-Ka
1611 KJV (AV) | Gloss: thy God | God-of-you

Base Word: 𐤄𐤅𐤋𐤀 (Ah-La-Wa-Ha) (noun) (shortened spelling 𐤄𐤋𐤀) means a deity, or the Deity and is indexed to Strong's #433. 𐤄𐤋𐤀 is perhaps the singular form of 𐤌𐤉𐤄𐤋𐤀 (Ah-La-Ha-Ya-Ma) (Strong's #430) which means "gods in the ordinary sense; [plural or with the article] the supreme God; [plural refers to:] human or divine rulers, judges, magistrates, representatives at sacred places or as reflecting

divine majesty or power, super human beings such as God and angels; the sons of God or the sons of god = angels; god, goddess".

𐤀𐤋𐤄 is a Hebrew name for "God" that corresponds to the Aramaic elahh (Strong's #426). The origin of the term is unknown. 𐤀𐤋𐤄 is a divine name in the Book of Job but it is rarely used as such in other Bible books. Brown-Driver-Brigg's: rulers, judges, divine ones, angels, gods, god, goddess, godlike one, works or special possessions of God, the (*true*) God, God.

Suffix(es): 𐤌𐤉 (Ya-Ma) tells us that the gender of 𐤀𐤋𐤄 (shortened spelling of 𐤀𐤋𐤅𐤄) is masculine and its number is plural.

𐤊 (Ka) is the 2nd person, masculine, singular possessive pronoun "[of] you", "your".

Explanation: Here is how this word is constructed:

Step 1: Base word 𐤀𐤋𐤄 (Ah-La-Ha) (noun) + plural suffix 𐤌𐤉 (Ya-Ma) + suffix 𐤊 (Ka) (2nd person, masculine, singular possessive pronoun)

Step 2: Because 𐤀𐤋𐤄𐤉𐤌 is in the construct state, the 𐤌 in 𐤌𐤉 (Ya-Ma) must be deleted as shown here 𐤊 + ~~𐤌~~𐤉 + 𐤀𐤋𐤄 which leaves 𐤊 + 𐤉 + 𐤀𐤋𐤄 (Ah-La-Ha-Ya-Ka) to form the word 𐤀𐤋𐤄𐤉𐤊.

Context always determines if the word 𐤀𐤋𐤄𐤉𐤊 (Ah-La-Ha-Ya-Ka) (noun) is singular or plural. 𐤀𐤋𐤄𐤉𐤊 describes 𐤉𐤄𐤅𐤄 (YHWH (YHVH)) which is singular, therefore, the noun 𝄞𐤋𐤄𐤋𐤀 is also singular.

Phoenician Hebrew Word: 𐤋𐤀
Transliteration: Ah-La
1611 KJV (AV) | Gloss: a God | God

Base Word: 𐤋𐤀 (Ah-La) (masculine, noun) means "God" and is indexed to Strong's #410. Brown-Driver-Brigg's Meanings: god, god-like one, mighty one, mighty men, men of rank, mighty heroes, angels, god, false god, (demons, imaginations), God, the one true God, Jehovah, mighty things in nature, strength, power.

Explanation: 𐤋𐤀 is the base word of 𐤄𐤅𐤋𐤀 (Ah-La-Wa-Ha) (Strong's #433). The plural form of 𐤄𐤋𐤀 is 𐤌𐤉𐤄𐤋𐤀 (Ah-La-Ha-Ya-Ma) (Strong's #430).

Phoenician Hebrew Word: 𐤀𐤍𐤒
Transliteration: Qa-Na-Ah
1611 KJV (AV) | Gloss: jealous | jealous

Word: 𐤀𐤍𐤒 (adjective) is indexed to Strong's #7067 and means "jealous", "envious", "zealous". Brown-Driver-Brigg's Meanings: jealous (only of God).

Explanation: 𐤀𐤍𐤒 describes the noun 𐤋𐤀 (Ah-La) that is written immediately before 𐤀𐤍𐤒.

Phoenician Hebrew Word: 𐤃𐤒𐤐
Transliteration: Pa-Qa-Da
1611 KJV (AV) | Gloss: visiting | visiting

Root Word: 𐤃𐤒𐤐 (verb) means to attend to, muster, reckon, visit, and is indexed to Strong's #6485. Brown-Driver-Brigg's Meanings: to attend to, muster, number, reckon, visit, punish, appoint, look after, care for; [verb form nuances:], observe, to seek, look about for, assign, lay upon as a charge, deposit, to be sought, be needed, to be visited upon, call up, to be passed in review, be caused to miss, be called, be called to account, to set over, make overseer, appoint an overseer, to commit, entrust, commit for care, to be deposited, numbered, expenses.

Phoenician Hebrew Word: 𐤏𐤅𐤍
Transliteration: I-Wa-Na
1611 KJV (AV) | Gloss: iniquities | inequity-of

Base Word: 𐤏𐤅𐤍 (I-Wa-Na) (masculine, noun) means iniquity, transgressions, sin, twisted one, and is indexed to Strong's #5771. Brown-Driver-Brigg's Meanings: perversity, depravity, iniquity, guilt or punishment of iniquity, consequence of or punishment for iniquity.

Explanation: Phoenician Hebrew nouns can be used as adjectives. When this occurs, add the suffix "ness" to the adjective when you render it. This rule does not work with every English word. For example, it does not work with the word transgression because "transgressionness" is not a word. Sin (sinfulness) and twisted (twistedness) are examples of words where the rule does work. It is you choice to apply this rule or not in your rendering.

Phoenician Hebrew Word: 𐤀𐤁𐤕
Transliteration: Ah-Ba-Tha
1611 KJV (AV) | Gloss: of the fathers | fathers

Word: 𐤀𐤁 (masculine, noun) is indexed to Strong's #1 and means "father". Brown-Driver-Brigg's Meanings: father of an individual, of God as father of his people, head or founder of a household, group, family, or clan, ancestor, grandfather, forefathers — of person, of people, originator or patron of a class, profession, or art, of producer, generator (figuratively), of benevolence and protection (figuratively), term of respect and honour, ruler or chief (specifically).

Suffix: ✗ (Tha) tells us that ᒍ✗ (Ah-Ba) (noun) is masculine and plural.

Explanation: ᒍ✗ (Ah-Ba) is a masculine plural noun. ᵞᒣ (Ya-Ma) is the masculine plural suffix. ✗ᵞ (Wa-Tha) and ✗ (Tha) are the feminine plural suffixes. So, why is the feminine plural suffix ✗ (Tha) attached to the masculine plural noun ᒍ✗? The answer is that ᒍ✗ is an ancient noun and in ancient times, the suffixes ✗ᵞ (Wa-Tha) and ✗ (Tha) were used to indicate masculine gender and plural number.

Explanation: ᒣᵞO (I-Wa-Na) and ✗ᒍ✗ (Ah-Ba-Tha) are nouns. When two nouns are next to each other they are said to be in the construct state. To render them in English, the word "of" must be inserted between them, thus—"transgressions of fathers"

Phoenician Hebrew Word: ᒣO
Transliteration: I-La
1611 KJV (AV) | Gloss: upon | on

Word: ᒣO (I-La) (preposition) means upon and is indexed to Strong's #5921. Brown-Driver-Brigg's Meanings: upon, on the ground of, according to, on account of, on behalf of, concerning, beside, in addition to, together with, beyond, above, over, by, on to, towards, to, against (preposition), down upon, upon, on, from, up upon, up to, towards, over towards, to, against (with verbs of motion).

Phoenician Hebrew Word: ᵞᒣᒍ
Transliteration: Ba-Na-Ya-Ma
1611 KJV (AV) | Gloss: children | children

Base Word: 𐤁𐤍 (masculine, noun) is indexed to Strong's #1121 and means "son". Brown-Driver-Brigg's Meanings: son, grandson, child, member of a group, son, male child, grandson, children (plural — male and female), youth, young men (plural), young (of animals), sons (as characterisation, i.e. sons of injustice [for unrighteous men] or sons of God [for angels]), people (of a nation), of lifeless things, i.e. sparks, stars, arrows (figuratively), a member of a guild, order, class.

Suffix: 𐤌𐤉 (Ya-Ma) tells us that 𐤁𐤍 (noun) is masculine and plural.

Phoenician Hebrew Word: 𐤏𐤋
Transliteration: I-La
1611 KJV (AV) | Gloss: upon | on

Word: 𐤏𐤋 is a preposition indexed to Strong's #5921 and means "upon". Brown-Driver-Brigg's Meanings: upon, on the ground of, according to, on account of, on behalf of, concerning, beside, in addition to, together with, beyond, above, over, by, on to, towards, to, against (preposition), down upon, upon, on, from, up upon, up to, towards, over towards, to, against (with verbs of motion).

Phoenician Hebrew Word: 𐤔𐤋𐤔𐤌𐤉
Transliteration: Sha-La-Sha-Ya-Ma
1611 KJV (AV) | Gloss: the third | ones-of-third

Base Word: 𐤔𐤋𐤔 means "pertaining to the third [generation]" and is indexed to Strong's #8029.

Suffix: 𐤌𐤉 (Ya-Ma) tells us that 𐤔𐤋𐤔𐤌𐤉 (Sha-La-Sha) (noun) is plural.

Phoenician Hebrew Word: 𐤅𐤏𐤋

Transliteration: Wa-I-La
1611 KJV (AV) | Gloss: and | and-on

Base Word: W𝘓W (preposition) means "upon" and is indexed to Strong's #5921. Brown-Driver-Brigg's Meanings: upon, on the ground of, according to, on account of, on behalf of, concerning, besides, in addition to, together with, beyond, above, over, by, on to, towards, to, against (preposition).

Prefix(es): ↑ (Wa) is the conjunction "and".

Phoenician Hebrew Word: ⚶𝟤O⌁⚶
Transliteration: Ra-Ba-I-Ya-Ma
1611 KJV (AV) | Gloss: fourth generation | ones-of-fourth

Base Word: O⌁⚶ (masculine, noun) means "pertaining to the fourth [generation]" and is indexed to Strong's #7256.

Suffix: ⚶𝟤 (Ya-Ma) tells us that ⚶𝟤O⌁⚶ (Ra-Ba-I-Ya-Ma) is plural.

Phoenician Hebrew Word: 𝟤⚶⌁W𝘓
Transliteration: La-Sha-Na-Ah-Ya
1611 KJV (AV) | Gloss: of them that hate me | to-ones-hating-of-me.

Root Word: ⚶⌁W (Sha-Na-Ah) (verb) means hate and occurs in the participle form (hating). ⚶⌁W (Sha-Na-Ah) is indexed to Strong's #8130. Brown-Driver-Brigg's Meanings: to hate, be hateful, [verb form nuances:] to hate, of man, of God, hater, one hating, enemy (participle) (substantive), to be hated, hater (participle), [hater] of persons, nations, God, wisdom.

Prefix: 𝘓 (La) is the preposition "for".

Suffix: ⚶𝟤 (Ya-Ma) tells us that the subject of the verb 𝟤⚶⌁W𝘓 (La-Sha-Na-Ah-Ya) is plural—"for them that hate" or "of those hating".

𝒴 (Ya) tells us that the object of 𝒴 ⚹ 𝟕 W ℓ is the 1st person, singular, pronoun "me", thus this word is rendered—"of them that hate me" or "of those hating me".

Explanation: Here is how 𝒴 ⚹ 𝟕 W ℓ (La-Sha-Na-Ah-Ya) is constructed:

Step 1: ⚹ 𝟕 W (Sha-Na-Ah) (root word) + ℓ (La) (prefix, preposition) + 𝒴𝒴 (Ya-Ma) (suffix, plural) + 𝒴 (Ya) (suffix, 1st person, pronoun) forms 𝒴𝒴 𝒴 ⚹ 𝟕 W ℓ

Step 2: Because the this plural verb 𝒴 ⚹ 𝟕 W ℓ occurs in the construct state, the 𝒴 must be deleted as shown here ℓ + ⚹ 𝟕 W + ~~𝒴~~ + 𝒴, which leaves ℓ + ⚹ 𝟕 W + 𝒴 + 𝒴

Step 3: Any double pictographs must be combined, thus ℓ + ⚹ 𝟕 W + 𝒴 + 𝒴 becomes ℓ + ⚹ 𝟕 W + 𝒴, which forms the word 𝒴 ⚹ 𝟕 W ℓ.

Write your own literal translation of Exodus 20:5 in the space below:

Ancient Script: _____
_____
_____
_____

Paleo Script: _____
_____
_____
_____

Exodus 20:6

𐤋𐤀𐤇𐤓𐤉𐤌 · 𐤋𐤀𐤉𐤔𐤌𐤓𐤉 · 𐤋𐤀𐤁𐤄𐤁𐤉 · 𐤋𐤀𐤋𐤐𐤉𐤌 · 𐤇𐤎𐤃 · 𐤄𐤔𐤏𐤉
my Commandements   and keepe   of them that loue mee vnto thousands   mercy   and showing

And shewing mercy vnto thousands of them that loue mee, and keepe my Commandements.

Phoenician Hebrew Word: 𐤄𐤔𐤏𐤉
Transliteration: Wa-I-Sha-Ha
1611 KJV (AV) | Gloss: and showing | but-doing

Root Word: 𐤄𐤔𐤏 (I-Sha-Ha) (verb) means "do", "make" and is indexed to Strong's #6213. Brown-Driver-Brigg's Meanings: to do, fashion, accomplish, make, work, produce, to deal (with), to act, act with effect, effect, to make, to produce, to prepare, to make (an offering), to attend to, put in order, to observe, celebrate, to acquire (property), to appoint, ordain, institute, to bring about, to use, to spend, pass.

Prefix: 𐤉 (Wa) is the conjunction "and". Depending on the context, some translators render 𐤉 as "but". What potential problems might this present?
Explanation: Always consider the context when rendering words into English.

Phoenician Hebrew Word: 𐤇𐤎𐤃
Transliteration: Chaa-Sa-Da
1611 KJV (AV) | Gloss: mercy | steadfast love

Word: 𐤇𐤎𐤃 (Chaa-Sa-Da) (noun) refers to the mutual and reciprocal rights, duties and obligations between two parties. It is indexed to Strong's #2617 and means "kindness", "steadfastness", "love". 𐤇𐤎𐤃 cannot be adequately rendered by any one of the above words alone. Brown-Driver-Brigg's Meanings: goodness, kindness, faithfulness, a reproach, shame.

Phoenician Hebrew Word: 𐤋𐤀𐤋𐤐𐤉𐤌
Transliteration: La-Ah-La-Pa-Ya-Ma
1611 KJV (AV) | Gloss: unto thousands | to thousands

Base Word: 𐤀𐤋𐤐 (Ah-La-Na) (masculine, noun) is indexed to Strong's #505 and means "thousands". Brown-Driver-Brigg's Meanings: a thousand, as numeral, a thousand, company, as a company of men under one leader, troops.

Prefix: 𐤋 (La) is the preposition "to" or "to the".

Suffix: 𐤉𐤌 (Ya-Ma) tells us that 𐤋𐤀𐤋𐤐𐤉𐤌 (La-Ah-Pa-Ya-Ma) is plural.

Phoenician Hebrew Word: 𐤋𐤀𐤄𐤁𐤉
Transliteration: La-Ah-Ha-Ba-Ya
1611 KJV (AV) | Gloss: of them that love me | to-ones-loving-of-me

Root Word: 𐤀𐤄𐤁 (Ah-Ha-Ba) (verb, participle form) means love, loving, and is indexed to Strong's #157. Brown-Driver-Brigg's Meanings: to love; [verb form nuances:] human love for another, includes family, and sexual, human appetite for objects such as food, drink, sleep, wisdom, human love for or to God, act of being a friend, lover (participle), friend (participle), God's love toward man, to individual men to people Israel, to righteousness, lovers (figuratively of adulterers), to like.

Prefix: 𐤋 (La) is the preposition "for".

Suffix: 𐤉𐤌 (Ya-Ma) tells us that the subject of the verb 𐤀𐤄𐤁 (Ah-Ha-Ba) is plural, thus 𐤋𐤀𐤄𐤁𐤉𐤌 means "[for] of them that love", "for the ones loving" and "for those who love". (See the Explanation below regarding how this suffix 𐤉𐤌 (Ya-Ma) changes in the construction of this word).

The suffix 𝄞 (Ya) tells us that the object of the verb 𐤀𐤄𐤁 is the 1st person, singular, pronoun "me", thus 𐤋𐤀𐤄𐤁𐤉 (La-Ah-Ha-Ba-Ya) means "[for] of them that love me", "for the ones loving me", etc.

Explanation: Here's how 𐤋𐤀𐤄𐤁𐤉 is constructed:

Step 1: the root word 𐤀𐤄𐤁 (Ah-Ha-Ba) (verb, participle form) + the prefix 𐤋 (La) (preposition) + the suffix 𐤌𐤉 (Ya-Ma) (plural) + the 1st person pronoun suffix 𐤉 (Ya), which forms 𐤋𐤀𐤄𐤁𐤉𐤌𐤉

Step 2: Because 𐤋𐤀𐤄𐤁𐤉 is written in the construct state, the 𐤌 in 𐤌𐤉 must be deleted as shown here 𐤋𐤀𐤄𐤁𐤉~~𐤌~~𐤉, which leaves 𐤉 + 𐤉 + 𐤀𐤄𐤁 + 𐤋

Step 3: Any double pictographs must be combined, thus the 𐤉 + 𐤉 must be reduced to a single 𐤉 as shown here 𐤉 + 𐤀𐤄𐤁 + 𐤋 which forms the word 𐤋𐤀𐤄𐤁𐤉 (La-Ah-Ha-Ba-Ya).

Phoenician Hebrew Word: 𐤉𐤌𐤔𐤋𐤅
Transliteration: Wa-La-Sha-Ma-Ra-Ya
1611 KJV (AV) | Gloss: and keep | and-to-ones-keeping-of

Root Word: 𐤌𐤔 (verb) means "guard", "guarding" and is indexed to Strong's #8104. Brown-Driver-Brigg's Meanings: to keep, guard, observe, give heed; [verb form nuances:] have charge of, keep watch and ward, protect, save life, watch, watchman (participle), to watch for, wait for, to watch, observe, to keep, retain, treasure up (in memory), to keep (within bounds), restrain, to observe, celebrate, keep (sabbath or covenant or commands), perform (vow), to be on one's guard, take heed, take care, beware, to keep oneself, refrain, abstain, to be kept, be guarded, to keep, pay heed, to keep oneself from.

Prefix: 𐤅 (Wa) is the conjunction "and". 𐤋 (La) is the preposition "for".

Suffix: 𐤌𐤉 (Ya-Ma) tells us that the subject of the verb 𐤔𐤌𐤓 (Sha-Ma-Ra) is plural.

Explanation: Here's how 𐤉𐤓𐤌𐤔𐤋𐤅 (Wa-La-Sha-Ma-Ra-Ya) is constructed:

Step 1: 𐤔𐤌𐤓 (root word, verb) + 𐤅 (Wa) (prefix, conjunction) + 𐤋 (La) (prefix, preposition) + 𐤌𐤉 (Ya-Ma) (plural, suffix)

Step 2: Because this plural verb 𐤉𐤓𐤌𐤔𐤋𐤅 occurs in the construct state, the 𐤌 (Ma) in the plural suffix 𐤌𐤉 must be deleted as shown here ̶𐤌̶𐤉 + 𐤔𐤌𐤓 + 𐤋 + 𐤅, which leaves 𐤉 + 𐤔𐤌𐤓 + 𐤋 + 𐤅 to form the word 𐤉𐤓𐤌𐤔𐤋𐤅.

Phoenician Hebrew Word: 𐤉𐤄𐤅𐤑𐤌
Transliteration: Ma-Taza-Wa-Tha-Ya
1611 KJV (AV) | Gloss: my commandments | commandments-of-me

Base Word: 𐤄𐤅𐤑𐤌 (Ma-Taza-Wa-Ha) (feminine, plural, noun) means commandments and is indexed to Strong's #4687. Brown-Driver-Brigg's Meanings: commandment (*of man*), the commandment (*of God*), commandment (*of code of wisdom*).

Suffix: 𐤄 (Tha) tells us that this base word 𐤄𐤅𐤑𐤌 (Ma-Taza-Wa-Ha) (noun) is plural, thus it means "commandments". The 𐤉 (Ya) is the 1st person, singular, possessive pronoun "[of] me" or "my".

Explanation: Here's how 𐤉𐤄𐤅𐤑𐤌 (Ma-Taza-Wa-Tha-Ya) is

constructed:

Step 1: The base word ᗏᔭᕁᢅ (Ma-Taza-Wa-Ha) (feminine, noun) + the suffix ᕁᔭ (Wa-Tha) (plural) + the suffix ᒉ (Ya) (possessive, pronoun)

Step 2: When the plural suffix ᕁᔭ (Wa-Tha) is attached to a feminine noun whose last pictograph is the ᗏ (Ha), something interesting happens! The ᗏ (Ha) is deleted from the feminine noun as shown here ᗏ̶ᔭᕁᢅ (Ma-Taza-Wa-H̶a̶). What remains is ᒉ+ᕁᔭ+ᔭᕁᢅ

Step 3: The feminine, plural suffix ᕁᔭ (Wa-Tha) is reduced to ᕁ (Tha), by convention, as shown here ᕁ̶ᔭ̶, which leaves ᒉ+ᕁ+ᔭᕁᢅ to form the word ᒉᕁᔭᕁᢅ (Ma-Taza-Wa-Tha-Ya).

Write your own literal translation of Exodus 20:6 in the space below:

Ancient Script: _____
_____
_____
_____

Paleo Script: _____
_____
_____
_____

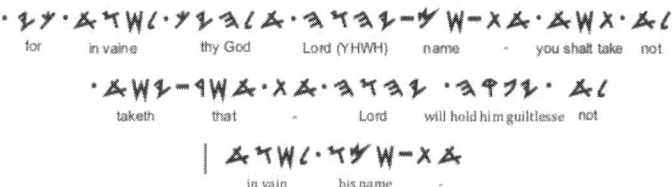

Thou shalt not take the Name of the Lord thy God in vaine: for the Lord will not holde him guiltlesse, that taketh his Name in vaine.

Phoenician Hebrew Word: 𐤀𐤋
Transliteration: La-Ah
1611 KJV (AV) | Gloss: not | not

Word: 𐤀𐤋 (negative participle) is indexed to Strong's #3808 and means "not". Brown-Driver-Brigg's Meanings: not, no, not (with verb — absolute prohibition), not (with modifier — negation), nothing (substantive), without (with particle), before (of time).

Explanation: 𐤀𐤋 negates the action of the verb that comes immediately after it. Stated another way, 𐤀𐤋 negates the action of the verb it is associated with.

Phoenician Hebrew Word: 𐤀𐤔𐤕
Transliteration: Tha-Sha-Ah
1611 KJV (AV) | Gloss: thou shalt take, | you-shall-take-up

Root Word: 𐤀𐤔𐤍 (Na-Sha-Ah) (verb) means "lift up, bear, carry, take" and is indexed to Strong's #5375.

Prefix: 𐤕 (Tha) tells us that the verb 𐤀𐤔𐤍 (Na-Sha-Na) is in the imperfect tense. 𐤕 (Tha) also tells us that the subject of the verb 𐤀𐤔𐤍 is the 2nd person, masculine, singular, pronoun "you", thus 𐤀𐤔𐤕 (Tha-Sha-Ah) means "you will lift up".

Explanation: When conjugating a verb that begin with 𐤍 (Na), the 𐤍 must be deleted as shown here 𐤀𐤔𐤍𐤕 which leaves 𐤀𐤔𐤕 (Tha-Sha-Ah). Due to the presence of the negative participle 𐤀𐤋 (La-Ah), the meaning of 𐤀𐤔𐤕 changes to "you will not lift up".

Phoenician Hebrew Word: 𐤕𐤀
Transliteration: Ah-Tha
1611 KJV (AV) | Gloss: untranslated

Word: 𐤕𐤀 (Ah-Tha) (untranslated, particle, direct object pointer) is indexed at Strong's #853 and always written before the definite direct object of the last verb. Brown-Driver-Brigg's Meanings: sign of the definite direct object, not translated in English but generally preceding and indicating the accusative.

Phoenician Hebrew Word: 𐤌𐤔
Transliteration: Sha-Ma
1611 KJV (AV) | Gloss: name | name-of

Base Word: 𐤌𐤔 (masculine, noun) and means appellation, reputation, memorial, personally identifying mark and is indexed to Strong's #8034. Brown-Driver-Brigg's Meanings: name, reputation, fame, glory, the Name (as designation of God)), memorial, monument.

Phoenician Hebrew Word: 𐤄𐤅𐤄𐤉
Transliteration: Ya-Ha-Wa-Ha
1611 KJV (AV) | Gloss: Lord | Yahweh

Root Word: 𐤄𐤅𐤄 (Ha-Wa-Ha) (verb) means "to fall out, come to pass, become, be" and is indexed to Strong's #1961. Brown-Driver-Brigg's Meanings: to be, become, come to pass, exist, happen, fall out, [verb form nuances:] to happen, fall out, occur, take place, come about, come to pass, to come about, come to pass, to come into being, become, to arise, appear, come, to become, to become, to become like, to be instituted, be established, to be, to exist, be in existence, to abide, remain, continue (with word of place or time), to stand, lie, be in, be at, be situated (with word of locality), to accompany, be with, to occur, come to pass, be done, be brought about, to be done, be finished, be gone.

Prefix: 𐤋 (Ya) tells us that the subject of the verb 𐤄𐤅𐤄 (Ha-Wa-Ha) is the 3rd person, masculine, singular, pronoun "he", thus 𐤄𐤅𐤄𐤋 means "he exists" or any of the various meanings given above. Of course, context is always helpful to determine a word's meaning and how to render it in English.

Explanation: Jewish people have a tradition of saying "adonai" (Strong's #136) when they read the name 𐤄𐤅𐤄𐤋 (YHWH (YHVH)). The Modern Hebrew vowel pointings in 𐤄𐤅𐤄𐤋 come from the vowel pointings in the word "adonai". The vowels are based on Jewish traditions and have nothing to do with the original pronunciation of 𐤄𐤅𐤄𐤋.

Following the Greek custom, Jewish grammarians combined the present and future tenses of the ancient Phoenician Hebrew Language into one tense (the Imperfect tense). For example, the words Ahayah and YHWH (YHVH) are merely different tenses of the same verb, "hayah" (Strong's #1961). What are the present and future tense conjugations of the verb hayah and what are there meanings? Why is YHWH (YHVH) considered a divine name? There is much more to this topic! Do you want to know more? If yes, Zion Law School will teach you all there is to know, grammatically, about the divines. Visit us online at zionlawschool.org and enroll in the 503 Biblical Hebrew Translations Skills class and the 504 Ten Commandments class. We are looking forward to seeing you in class!

Phoenician Hebrew Word: 𐤊𐤉𐤄𐤋𐤀
Transliteration: Ah-La-Ha-Ya-Ka
1611 KJV (AV) | Gloss: thy God | God-of-you

Base Word: 𐤄𐤅𐤋𐤀 (Ah-La-Wa-Ha) (noun) (shortened spelling 𐤄𐤋𐤀) means a deity, or the Deity and is indexed to Strong's #433. 𐤄𐤅𐤋𐤀 is perhaps the singular form of 𐤊𐤉𐤄𐤋𐤀 (Ah-La-Ha-Ya-Ma) (Strong's #430) and means "gods in the ordinary sense; [plural or with the article] the supreme God; [plural refers to:] human or divine rulers, judges, magistrates, representatives at sacred places or as reflecting divine majesty or power, super human beings such as God and angels; the sons of God or the sons of god = angels; god, goddess".

𐤄𐤋𐤀 is a Hebrew name for "God" that corresponds to the Aramaic elahh (Strong's #426). The origin of the term is unknown. 𐤄𐤋𐤀 is a divine name in the Book of Job but it is rarely used as such in other Bible books. Brown-Driver-Brigg's: rulers, judges, divine ones, angels, gods, god, goddess, godlike one, works or special possessions of God, the (true) God, God.

Suffix(es): 𐤉𐤌 (Ya-Ma) tells us that the gender of 𐤄𐤋𐤀 (shortened spelling of 𐤄𐤅𐤋𐤀) is masculine and its number is plural.

𐤊 (Ka) is the 2nd person, masculine, singular possessive pronoun "[of] you", "your".

Explanation: Here is how 𐤊𐤉𐤄𐤋𐤀 (Ah-La-Ha-Ya-Ka) is constructed:

Step 1: Base word 𐤄𐤋𐤀 (Ah-La-Ha) (noun) + plural suffix 𐤉𐤌 (Ya-Ma) + suffix 𐤊 (Ka) (2nd person, masculine, singular possessive pronoun)

Step 2: Because 𝕐𝕃𝔸𝕃𝔸 is in the construct state, the 𝕐 in 𝕐𝕐 (Ya-Ma) must be deleted as shown here 𝕐 + ~~𝕐~~ + 𝔸𝕃𝔸 which leaves 𝕐 + 𝕐 + 𝔸𝕃𝔸 (Ah-La-Ha-Ya-Ka) to form the word 𝕐𝕃𝔸𝕃𝔸.

Context always determines if the word 𝕐𝕃𝔸𝕃𝔸 (Ah-La-Ha-Ya-Ka) (noun) is singular or plural. 𝕐𝕃𝔸𝕃𝔸 describes 𝔸𝕐𝔸𝕃 (YHWH (YHVH)) which is singular, therefore, the noun 𝕐𝕃𝔸𝕃𝔸 is also singular.

When rendered in English, 𝕐W * 𝔸𝕐𝔸𝕃 * 𝕐𝕃𝔸𝕃𝔸 forms the phrase, "name of [the] Lord thy God", "name of YHWH (YHVH) your God", "name of God of you". This phrase, is the definite direct object of the verb 𝔸W𝕏 (Tha-Sha-Ah) ("you will lift up"). Why? Because 𝔸W𝕏 (Tha-Sha-Ah) is the last verb that occurred before this phrase.

Phoenician Hebrew Word: 𝔸𝕐W𝕃
Transliteration: La-Sha-Wa-Ah
1611 KJV (AV) | Gloss: in vain | for-the-vanity

Base Word: 𝔸𝕐W (Sha-Wa-Ah) (masculine, noun) means lying, emptiness of speech, emptiness, nothingness, false, vanity, vain, and is indexed to Strong's #7723. Brown-Driver-Brigg's Meanings: emptiness, vanity, falsehood, emptiness, nothingness, vanity, emptiness of speech, lying, worthlessness (of conduct).

Prefix: 𝕃 (La) is the preposition "to" and "as".

Phoenician Hebrew Word: 𐤊𐤉
Transliteration: Ka-Ya
1611 KJV (AV) | Gloss: for | for

Word: 𐤊𐤉 (conjunction) means because and is indexed to Strong's #3588. Brown-Driver-Brigg's Meanings: that, for, because, when, as though, as, because that, but, then, certainly, except, surely, since.

Phoenician Hebrew Word: 𐤋𐤀
Transliteration: La-Ah

1611 KJV (AV) | Gloss: not | not **Word**: 𐤋𐤀 (negative participle) means not and is indexed to Strong's #3808. Brown-Driver-Brigg's Meanings: not, no, not (with verb — absolute prohibition), not (with modifier — negation), nothing (substantive), without (with particle), before (of time).

Explanation: 𐤋𐤀 negates the action of the verb that comes immediately after it. Stated another way, 𐤋𐤀 negates the action of the verb it is associated with.

Phoenician Hebrew Word: 𐤉𐤍𐤒𐤄
Transliteration: Ya-Na-Qa-Ha
1611 KJV (AV) | Gloss: hold him guiltless | he-will-hold-guiltless

Root Word: 𐤍𐤒𐤄 (verb) means acquit and is indexed to Strong's #5352.

Prefix: 𐤉 (Ya) tells us that 𐤉𐤍𐤒𐤄 (Ya-Na-Qa-Ha) is written in the imperfect tense. 𐤉 also tells us that the subject of this verb is the 3rd person, masculine, singular "he", thus "he will acquit".

Explanation: The presence of the negative participle 𐤋𐤀 (La-

Ah) negates the action of 𐤀𐤐𐤍, thus its meaning changes to "he will not acquit".

Phoenician Hebrew Word: 𐤄𐤅𐤄𐤉
Transliteration: Ya-Ha-Wa-Ha
1611 KJV (AV) | Gloss: Lord, Yahweh

Root Word: 𐤄𐤅𐤄 (Ha-Wa-Ha) (verb) means "to fall out, come to pass, become, be" and is indexed to Strong's #1961. Brown-Driver-Brigg's Meanings: to be, become, come to pass, exist, happen, fall out, [verb form nuances:] to happen, fall out, occur, take place, come about, come to pass, to come about, come to pass, to come into being, become, to arise, appear, come, to become, to become, to become like, to be instituted, be established, to be, to exist, be in existence, to abide, remain, continue (with word of place or time), to stand, lie, be in, be at, be situated (with word of locality), to accompany, be with, to occur, come to pass, be done, be brought about, to be done, be finished, be gone.

Prefix: 𐤉 (Ya) tells us that the subject of the verb 𐤄𐤅𐤄 (Ha-Wa-Ha) is the 3rd person, masculine, singular, pronoun "he", thus 𐤄𐤅𐤄𐤉 means "he exists" or any of the various meanings given above. Of course, context is always helpful to determine a word's meaning and how to render it in English.

Explanation: Jewish people have a tradition of saying "adonai" (Strong's #136) when they read the name 𐤄𐤅𐤄𐤉 (YHWH (YHVH)). The Modern Hebrew vowel pointings in 𐤄𐤅𐤄𐤉 come from the vowel pointings in the word "adonai". The vowels are based on Jewish traditions and have nothing to do with the original pronunciation of 𐤄𐤅𐤄𐤉.

Following the Greek custom, Jewish grammarians combined the present and future tenses of the ancient Phoenician Hebrew Language into one tense (the Imperfect tense). For example, the words Ahayah and YHWH (YHVH) are merely different tenses of the same verb, "hayah" (Strong's #1961). What are the present and future tense conjugations of the verb hayah and what are there meanings? Why is YHWH (YHVH) considered a divine name? There is much more to this topic! Do you want to know more? If yes, Zion Law School will teach you all there is to know, grammatically, about the divines. Visit us online at zionlawschool.org and enroll in the 503 Biblical Hebrew Translations Skills class and the 504 Ten Commandments class. We are looking forward to seeing you in class!

Phoenician Hebrew Word: X A
Transliteration: Ah-Tha
1611 KJV (AV) | Gloss: untranslated

Word: X A (untranslated, particle, direct object pointer) is indexed at Strong's #853 and always written before the definite direct object of the last verb. Brown-Driver-Brigg's Meanings: sign of the definite direct object, not translated in English but generally preceding and indicating the accusative.

Phoenician Hebrew Word: 1W A
Transliteration: Ah-Sha-Ra
1611 KJV (AV) | Gloss: that | who

Word: 1W A (Ah-Sha-Ra) (genderless, numberless, relative participle) means "who, what, which, that" and is indexed to Strong's #834. Brown-Driver-Brigg's Meanings: (relative participle), which, who, that, which.

Phoenician Hebrew Word: A W Y
Transliteration: Ya-Sha-Ah
1611 KJV (AV) | Gloss: takes | he-takes-up

Root Word: 1W Y (Na-Sha-Ah) (verb) means lift up, and is indexed to Strong's #5375.

Prefix: 𝒴 (Ya) tells us that ᴀWᵥ (Ya-Sha-Ah) (verb) is in the imperfect tense. 𝒴 also tells us that the subject of ᴀWᵥ (verb) is the 3ⁿᵈ person, masculine, singular, pronoun "he"—the "he" in "he will lift up".

Explanation: When conjugating a *verb* whose first pictograph is the 𝟕 (Na), the 𝟕 must be deleted as shown here 𝟕̷ ᴀWᵥ (N̶a̶-Ya-Sha-Ah). Due to the presence of the negative participle ᴀℓ (La-Ah), ᴀWᵥ is rendered "you will not lift up".

Phoenician Hebrew Word: ✕ᴀ
Transliteration: Ah-Tha
1611 KJV (AV) | Gloss: untranslated

Word: ✕ᴀ (untranslated, particle, direct object pointer) and is indexed at Strong's #853 and is always written before the definite direct object of the last verb. Brown-Driver-Brigg's Meanings: sign of the definite direct object, not translated in English but generally preceding and indicating the accusative.

Phoenician Hebrew Word: ʈᵧW
Transliteration: Sha-Ma-Wa
1611 KJV (AV) | Gloss: his name | name-of-him

Base Word: ᵧW (Sha-Ma) (masculine, noun) means appellation, reputation, memorial, personally identifying mark and is indexed to Strong's #8034. Brown-Driver-Brigg's Meanings: name, reputation, fame, glory, the Name (as designation of God), memorial, monument.

Suffix: ʈ (Wa) is the 3ʳᵈ person, masculine, singular possessive pronoun "his", "of him", thus ʈᵧW means "his name", "name of him", etc.

Explanation: ⟨Sha-Ma-Wa⟩ is the second definite direct object of the verb that occurred immediately before it. In other words, ⟨Sha-Ma-Wa⟩ is the second direct object of the verb ⟨Ya-Sha-Ah⟩. Why? Because ⟨Ya-Sha-Ah⟩ is the last verb that occurred before the word ⟨Sha-Ma-Wa⟩.

Phoenician Hebrew Word: ⟨La-Sha-Wa-Ah⟩
Transliteration: La-Sha-Wa-Ah
1611 KJV (AV) | Gloss: in vain | for-the-vanity

Base Word: ⟨Sha-Wa-Ah⟩ (masculine, noun) is indexed to Strong's #7723 and means "false". Brown-Driver-Brigg's Meanings: emptiness, vanity, falsehood, nothingness, vanity, emptiness of speech, lying, worthlessness (of conduct).

Prefix: ⟨La⟩ is the preposition "to" and "as", thus ⟨La-Sha-Wa-Ah⟩ means "[in] vain" "as nothingness", "as worthlessness", "as vanity", etc.

Write your own literal translation of Exodus 20:7 in the space below:

Ancient Script: _____
_____
_____
_____

Paleo Script: _____
_____
_____
_____
_____
_____
_____

Exodus: 20:8

| 𐤏𐤔𐤃𐤒𐤋·𐤕𐤉𐤔𐤁·𐤌𐤅𐤉-𐤕𐤀·𐤇𐤊𐤆 |
| to keepe it holy   Sabbath   day   ·   remember |

Remember the Sabbath day, to keepe it holy.

Phoenician Hebrew Word: 𐤇𐤊𐤆
Transliteration: Za-Ka-Wa-Ra
1611 KJV (AV) | Gloss: remember | to-remember

Root Word: 𐤊𐤆 (Za-Ka-Ra) (verbal noun) is indexed to Strong's #2142 and means "remember". Brown-Driver-Brigg's Meanings: to remember, recall, to record, to make a memorial.

Explanation: Verbal nouns have features in common with verbs and nouns, and are generally translated with the preposition "to", thus "to remember". Like a noun, verbal nouns can function as a subject (to remember the Sabbath) or an object (I want to remember) of a verb.

Phoenician Hebrew Word: 𐤕𐤀
Transliteration: Ah-Tha
1611 KJV (AV) | Gloss: untranslated

Word: 𐤕𐤀 (untranslated, particle, direct object pointer) is indexed at Strong's #853 and is always written before the definite direct object of the last verb. Brown-Driver-Brigg's Meanings: sign of the definite direct object, not translated in English but generally preceding and indicating the accusative.

Explanation: Phoenician Hebrew verbs have both a subject and an object. Recall that the last verb in this verse was 𐤇𐤊𐤆 (Za-Ka-Wa-Ra) which is rendered "to remember".

Phoenician Hebrew Word: 𐤌𐤅𐤉
Transliteration: Ya-Wa-Ma
1611 KJV (AV) | Gloss: day | day-of

Base Word: 𐤌𐤅𐤉 (Ya-Wa-Ma) (masculine, noun) means "day", "period of daylight" and is indexed to Strong's #3117. Brown-Driver-Brigg's Meanings: day, time, year, day (as opposed to night), day (24 hour period), as defined by evening and morning in Genesis as a division of time, a working day, a day's journey, days, lifetime, time, period (general), year, temporal references, today, yesterday, tomorrow.

Phoenician Hebrew Word: 𐤄𐤔𐤁𐤕
Transliteration: Ha-Sha-Ba-Tha
1611 KJV (AV) | Gloss: Sabbath | the-Sabbath

Base Word: 𐤔𐤁𐤕 (Sha-Ba-Tha) (noun) means "intermission, desist from exertion" and is indexed to Strong's #7676. Brown-Driver-Brigg's Meanings: Sabbath, sabbath, day of, atonement, sabbath year, week, produce (in sabbath year).

Prefix: 𐤄 (Ha) is the article "the".

Explanation: 𐤄𐤔𐤁𐤕 (Ha-Sha-Ba-Tha) (noun) means the intermission. Note that the noun 𐤄𐤔𐤁𐤕 (Ha-Sha-Ba-Tha) and the noun 𐤌𐤅𐤉 (Ya-Wa-Ma) are in the construct state. Why? Because the construct state is formed whenever two nouns occur next to each other. The word "of" must be inserted between them to render them in English, thus 𐤄𐤔𐤁𐤕 (Ha-Sha-Ba-Tha) * 𐤌𐤅𐤉 (Ya-Wa-Ma), are rendered "the day of intermission". Observe that the article (the) is transferred from in the front of the word "intermission" and placed in front of the word "day" in the rendering.

"The day of ceasing" is the definite direct object of 𐤋𐤒𐤃𐤔𐤅 (Za-Ka-Wa-Ra), which is the last verb in this verse.

Phoenician Hebrew Word: 𐤋𐤒𐤃𐤔𐤅
Transliteration: La-Qa-Da-Sha-Wa
1611 KJV (AV) | Gloss: to keep it holy | to-declare-holy-him

Root Word: 𐤒𐤃𐤔 (Qa-Da-Sha) (verb) means "set apart for a special purpose" and is indexed to Strong's #6942. Brown-Driver-Brigg's Meanings: to consecrate, sanctify, prepare, dedicate, be hallowed, be holy, be sanctified, be separate, [verb form nuances:] to be set apart, be consecrated, tabooed.

Prefix: 𐤋 (La) is the preposition "for".

Suffix: 𐤅 (Wa) tells us that the object of 𐤅𐤔𐤃𐤒𐤋 (La-Qa-Da-Sha-Wa) (verb) is the 3rd person, masculine, singular "him", which has reference to the word "day" 𐤌𐤅𐤉 (Ya-Wa-Ma) (masculine, noun).

Write your own literal translation of Exodus 20:8 in the space below:

Ancient Script: _____
_____
_____
_____

Paleo Script: _____
_____
_____
_____
_____

Exodus 20:9

| 𐤅𐤗𐤅𐤁𐤋𐤉-𐤋𐤊 𐤕𐤋𐤏𐤅𐤓 𐤃𐤏𐤏𐤗 𐤌𐤉𐤌𐤉 𐤗𐤔𐤔
| thy worke   all   and doe   shalt thou labour   dayes   sixe

Sixe dayes shalt thou labour, and doe all thy worke:

Phoenician Hebrew Word: 𐤗𐤔𐤔
Transliteration: Sha-Sha-Tha
1611 KJV (AV) | Gloss: sixe | six of

Word: 𐤀𐤔𐤔 (Sha-Sha-Ha) (adjective) is indexed to Strong's #8337 and means "six".

Explanation: Because the last pictograph in the root word 𐤀𐤔𐤔 (adjective) is the 𐤀 (Ha), the 𐤀 (Ha) must be deleted and replaced with the 𐤗 (Tha) as shown here 𐤗𐤀𐤔𐤔 (Sha-Sha-Ha-*Tha*), which leaves 𐤗𐤔𐤔.

Phoenician Hebrew, nouns and adjectives are interchangeable. In this verse, the adjective 𐤀𐤔𐤔 (Sha-Sha-Ha) is functioning like a noun. Why? Keep reading if you want to find out!

Here are the rules to determine if an adjective is functioning as a noun:

Rule 1) A Phoenician Hebrew adjective must occur after the noun it describes. In this case, 𐤀𐤔𐤔 occurs before the noun 𐤌𐤉𐤌𐤉 (Ya-Ma-Ya-Ma) it describes, so it cannot be an adjective, therefore, 𐤀𐤔𐤔 (Sha-Sha-Ha) is functioning as a noun.

Rule 2) The construct state cannot be formed with an adjective. In this case, according to Rule 1 above, 𐤀𐤔𐤔 (Sha-Sha-Ha) is noun and the word that occurs after it is the noun, 𐤌𐤉𐤌𐤉

(Ya-Ma-Ya-Ma), thus the construct state is present.

Rule 3) A Phoenician Hebrew adjective must agree in gender and number with the noun it describes. In this case, ℨWW is singular but the noun 𐤌𐤉𐤌𐤉 it describes is plural—they do not agree. Therefore, ℨWW is functioning as a noun.

Phoenician Hebrew Word: 𐤌𐤉𐤌𐤉
Transliteration: Ya-Ma-Ya-Ma
1611 KJV (AV) | Gloss: days | days
Base Word: 𐤌𐤅𐤉 (Ya-Wa-Ma) (masculine, noun) and means "day", "period of daylight" and is indexed to Strong's #3117. Brown-Driver-Brigg's Meanings: day, time, year, day (as opposed to night), day (24 hour period), as defined by evening and morning in Genesis as a division of time, a working day, a day's journey, days, lifetime, time, period (general), year, temporal references, today, yesterday, tomorrow.
Suffix: 𐤌𐤉 (Ya-Ma) tells us that Ya-Wa-Ma (noun) is plural.
Explanation: The noun 𐤌𐤉𐤌𐤉 (Ya-Ma-Ya-Ma) occurs next to the noun ΧWW (Sha-Sha-Tha), thus these two nouns are in the construct state. To render (days) 𐤌𐤉𐤌𐤉 * (sixe) ΧWW into English, insert the word "of" between them, which yields "six of [the] days".

Phoenician Hebrew Word: 𐤃𐤁𐤏𐤕
Transliteration: Tha-I-Ba-Da
1611 KJV (AV) | Gloss: shalt thy labour | you-shall-labor
Root Word: 𐤃𐤁𐤏 (I-Ba-Da) (verb) means serve and is indexed to Strong's #5647. Brown-Driver-Brigg's Meanings: to work, serve; [verb form nuances]: to labour, work, do work, to work

for another, serve another by labour, to serve as subjects, to serve (*God*), to serve (with Levitical service), to be worked, be tilled (of land), to make oneself a servant, to be worked, to compel to labour or work, cause to labour, cause to serve, to cause to serve as subjects, to be led or enticed to serve.

Prefix: ✗ (Tha) tells us that ◁𝟻O (I-Ba-Da) is written in the imperfect tense, "will serve". ✗ also tells us that the subject of ◁𝟻O (I-Ba-Da) is the 2nd person, masculine, singular, pronoun "you", thus ◁𝟻O✗ means "you will serve".

Phoenician Hebrew Word: ✗𝟻WO✝
Transliteration: Wa-I-Sha-Ya-Tha
1611 KJV (AV) | Gloss: and do | and-you-shall-do

Root Word: ⋺WO (I-Sha-Ha) (verb) means "do", "make" and is indexed to Strong's #6213. Brown-Driver-Brigg's Meanings: to do, fashion, accomplish, make, work, produce, to deal (with), to act, act with effect, effect, to make, to produce, to prepare, to make (an offering), to attend to, put in order, to observe, celebrate, to acquire (property), to appoint, ordain, institute, to bring about, to use, to spend, pass.

Prefix: ✝ (Wa) is the conjunction "and".

Suffix: ✗ (Tha) tells us that ✗𝟻WO✝ (Wa-I-Sha-Ya-Tha) is written in the perfect tense, "did". ✗ also tells us that the subject of ✗𝟻WO✝ (Wa-I-Sha-Ya-Tha) is the 2nd person, masculine, singular, pronoun "you", thus "you did".

Explanation: The prefix ✝ (Wa) reverses the tense of ✗𝟻WO✝ to the future tense, "you will do".

Phoenician Hebrew Word: ᒪƳ

Transliteration: Ka-La
1611 KJV (AV) | Gloss: all | all-of

Word: ℓ𝒴 (Ka-La) (masculine, singular, noun) means "any, all, complete, every" and is indexed to Strong's #3605. Brown-Driver-Brigg's Meanings: all, the whole, the whole of, any, each, every, anything, totality, everything.

Phoenician Hebrew Word: 𝒴 𝒳 𝒴 𝒜 ℓ 𝒴
Transliteration: Ma-La-Ah-Ka-Tha-Ka
1611 KJV (AV) | Gloss: your work | work-of-you

Base Word: ℷ 𝒴 𝒜 ℓ 𝒴 (Ma-La-Ah-Ka-Ha) (feminine, noun) means "business" and is indexed to Strong's #4399. Brown-Driver-Brigg's Meanings: occupation, business, property, work (something done or made), workmanship, service, use, public business, political, religious.

Explanation: When two nouns are in the construct state and one of them is a feminine noun whose last pictograph is the ℷ (Ha), the ℷ must be deleted as shown here 𝒳 ℷ̶ 𝒴 𝒜 ℓ 𝒴 (Ma-La-Ah-Ka-H̶a̶-Tha) and replaced with the 𝒳 (Tha), which in this case yields 𝒴 𝒳 𝒴 𝒜 ℓ 𝒴.

Write your own literal translation of Exodus 20:9 in the space below:

Ancient Script: _____
_____
_____

Paleo Script: _____
_____
_____
_____

Exodus 20:10

𐤉𐤅𐤌 · 𐤄𐤔𐤁𐤉𐤏𐤉 · 𐤔𐤁𐤕 · 𐤋𐤉𐤄𐤅𐤄 · 𐤀𐤋𐤄𐤉𐤊·
but day   the seventh   Sabbath   of Lord (YHWH)   thy God

𐤋𐤀-𐤕𐤏𐤔𐤄 · 𐤊𐤋-𐤌𐤋𐤀𐤊𐤄 · 𐤀𐤕𐤄 · 𐤅𐤁𐤍𐤊-𐤅𐤁𐤕𐤊 ·
not   thou shalt do   any   work   thou   nor thy son   nor thy daughter

| 𐤏𐤁𐤃𐤊 · 𐤅𐤀𐤌𐤕𐤊 · 𐤅𐤁𐤄𐤌𐤕𐤊 · 𐤅𐤂𐤓𐤊 · 𐤀𐤔𐤓 · 𐤁𐤔𐤏𐤓𐤉𐤊
thy manservant   thy maidservant   nor thy cattle   nor thy stranger   that   within thy gates

But the seuenth day is the Sabbath of the Lord thy God: in it thou shalt not doe any worke, thou, nor thy sonne, nor thy daughter, thy man seruant, nor thy mayd seruant, nor thy cattell, nor thy stranger that is within thy gates:

Phoenician Hebrew Word: 𐤅𐤉𐤅𐤌

Transliteration: Wa-Ya-Wa-Ma

1611 KJV (AV) | Gloss: but day | but-day-of

Base Word: 𐤉𐤅𐤌 (Ya-Wa-Ma) (masculine, noun) means "day", "period of daylight" and is indexed to Strong's #3117. Brown-Driver-Brigg's Meanings: day, time, year, day (as opposed to night), day (24 hour period), as defined by evening and morning in Genesis as a division of time, a working day, a day's journey, days, lifetime, time, period (general), year, temporal references, today, yesterday, tomorrow.

Prefix: 𐤅 (Wa) is the conjunction "and".

Phoenician Hebrew Word: 𐤄𐤔𐤁𐤉𐤏𐤉

Transliteration: Ha-Sha-Ba-Ya-I-Ya

1611 KJV (AV) | Gloss: the seventh | the seventh

Base Word: 𐤔𐤁𐤉𐤏𐤉 (Sha-Ba-Ya-I-Ya) (adjective) means "seventh" and is indexed to Strong's #7637.

Prefix: 𐤄 (Ha) is the article "the".

Explanation: The adjective 𐤄𐤔𐤁𐤉𐤏𐤉 (Ha-Sha-Ba-Ya-I-Ya) means "the seventh" and it describes the noun 𐤅𐤉𐤅𐤌 (Wa-Ya-Wa-Ma) which means "and day". These words are combined to form the phrase 𝀀𝀁𝀂𝀃𝀄 * 𝀅𝀆𝀇𝀈 "and day the seventh". This phrase is difficult to understand, so it is rendered in English as "and the seventh day". The 1611 KJV renders it "But the seuenth day".

Phoenician Hebrew Word: 𐤔𐤁𐤕
Transliteration: Sha-Ba-Tha
1611 KJV (AV) | Gloss: Sabbath | Sabbath
Base Word: 𐤔𐤁𐤕 (Sha-Ba-Tha) (noun) means "intermission, desist from exertion" and is indexed to Strong's #7676. Brown-Driver-Brigg's Meanings: Sabbath, sabbath, day of, atonement, sabbath year, week, produce (in sabbath year).

Phoenician Hebrew Word: 𐤋𐤉𐤄𐤅𐤄
Transliteration: La-Ya-Ha-Wa-Ha
1611 KJV (AV) | Gloss: of Lord | to-Yahweh
Root Word: 𐤄𐤅𐤄 (Ha-Wa-Ha) (verb) means "to fall out, come to pass, become, be" and is indexed to Strong's #1961. Brown-Driver-Brigg's Meanings: to be, become, come to pass, exist, happen, fall out, [verb form nuances:] to happen, fall out, occur, take place, come about, come to pass, to come about, come to pass, to come into being, become, to arise, appear, come, to become, to become like, to be instituted, be established, to be, to exist, be in existence, to abide, remain, continue (with word of place or time), to stand, lie, be in, be at, be situated (with word of locality), to accompany, be with, to occur, come to pass, be done, be brought about, to be done, be finished, be gone.

Prefix: 𐤉 (Ya) tells us that the subject of the verb 𐤄𐤅𐤄 (Ha-Wa-Ha) is the 3rd person, masculine, singular, pronoun "he", thus 𐤋𐤉𐤄𐤅𐤄 means "he will be", "he will exist, "he exists" or any of the various meanings' given above. Of course, context is always helpful to determine a word's meaning and how to render it in English.

Explanation: Jewish people have a tradition of saying "adonai" (Strong's #136) when they read the name ‎𐤄𐤅𐤄𐤉 (YHWH (YHVH)). The Modern Hebrew vowel pointings in ‎𐤄𐤅𐤄𐤉 come from the vowel pointings in the word "adonai". The vowels are based on Jewish traditions and have nothing to do with the original pronunciation of ‎𐤄𐤅𐤄𐤉.

Following the Greek custom, Jewish grammarians combined the present and future tenses of the ancient Phoenician Hebrew Language into one tense (the Imperfect tense). For example, the words Ahayah and YHWH (YHVH) are merely different tenses of the same verb, "hayah" (Strong's #1961). What are the present and future tense conjugations of the verb hayah and what are there meanings? Why is YHWH (YHVH) considered a divine name? There is much more to this topic! Do you want to know more? If yes, Zion Law School will teach you all there is to know, grammatically, about the divine names. Visit us online at zionlawschool.org and enroll in the 503 Biblical Hebrew Translations Skills class and the 504 Ten Commandments class. We are looking forward to seeing you in class!

Phoenician Hebrew Word: ‎𐤀𐤊𐤄𐤋𐤀
Transliteration: Ah-La-Ha-Ya-Ka
1611 KJV (AV) | Gloss: thy God | God-of-you

Base Word: ‎𐤀𐤋𐤅𐤄 (Ah-La-Wa-Ha) (noun) (shortened spelling ‎𐤀𐤋𐤄) means a deity, or the Deity and is indexed to Strong's #433. ‎𐤀𐤋𐤄 is perhaps the singular form of ‎𐤀𐤋𐤄𐤉𐤌 (Ah-La-Ha-Ya-Ma) (Strong's #430) and means "gods in the ordinary sense; [plural or with the article] the supreme God; [plural refers to:] human or divine rulers, judges, magistrates, representatives at sacred places or as reflecting

divine majesty or power, super human beings such as God and angels; the sons of God or the sons of god = angels; god, goddess".

𐤀𐤋𐤄 is a Hebrew name for "God" that corresponds to the Aramaic elahh (Strong's #426). The origin of the term is unknown. 𐤀𐤋𐤄 is a divine name in the Book of Job but it is rarely used as such in other Bible books. Brown-Driver-Brigg's: rulers, judges, divine ones, angels, gods, god, goddess, godlike one, works or special possessions of God, the (true) God, God.

Suffix(es): 𐤌𐤉 (Ya-Ma) tells us that the gender of 𐤀𐤋𐤄 (shortened spelling of 𐤀𐤋𐤄𐤉𐤌) is masculine and its number is plural.

𐤊 (Ka) is the 2nd person, masculine, singular possessive pronoun "[of] you", "your".

Explanation: Here is how 𐤀𐤋𐤄𐤉𐤊 (Ah-La-Ha-Ka) is constructed:

Step 1: Base word 𐤀𐤋𐤄 (Ah-La-Ha) (noun) + the plural suffix 𐤌𐤉 (Ya-Ma) + the suffix 𐤊 (Ka) (2nd person, masculine, singular possessive pronoun)

Step 2: Because 𐤀𐤋𐤄𐤉𐤌 is in the construct state, the 𐤌 in 𐤌𐤉 (Ya-Ma) must be deleted as shown here 𐤊 + ~~𐤌~~𐤉 + 𐤀𐤋𐤄 which leaves 𐤊 + 𐤉 + 𐤀𐤋𐤄 (Ah-La-Ha-Ya-Ka) to form the word 𐤀𐤋𐤄𐤉𐤊.

Context always determines if the word 𐤀𐤋𐤄𐤉𐤊 (Ah-La-Ha-Ya-Ka) (noun) is singular or plural. 𐤀𐤋𐤄𐤉𐤊 describes

𝕐𝕙𝕨𝕙 (YHWH (YHVH)) which is singular, therefore, the noun 𝕪𝕫𝕒𝕝𝕩 is also singular.

Phoenician Hebrew Word: 𐤀𐤋
Transliteration: La-Ah
1611 KJV (AV) | Gloss: not | not

Word: 𐤀𐤋 (negative participle) is indexed to Strong's #3808 and means "not". Brown-Driver-Brigg's Meanings: not, no, not (with verb — absolute prohibition), not (with modifier — negation), nothing (substantive), without (with particle), before (of time).

Explanation: 𐤀𐤋 negates the action of the verb that comes immediately after it. Stated another way, 𐤀𐤋 negates the action of the verb it is associated with.

Phoenician Hebrew Word: 𐤀𐤔𐤏𐤕
Transliteration: Tha-I-Sha-Ha
1611 KJV (AV) | Gloss: thou shalt | you-shall-do

Root Word: 𐤀𐤔𐤏 (I-Sha-Ha) (verb) means "do", "make" and is indexed to Strong's #6213. Brown-Driver-Brigg's Meanings: to do, fashion, accomplish, make, work, produce, to deal (with), to act, act with effect, effect, to make, to produce, to prepare, to make (an offering), to attend to, put in order, to observe, celebrate, to acquire (property), to appoint, ordain, institute, to bring about, to use, to spend, pass.

Prefix(es): 𐤕 (Tha) tells us that 𐤀𐤔𐤏 (I-Sha-Ha) is written in the imperfect tense, "will do". 𐤕 (Tha) also tells us that the subject of 𐤀𐤔𐤏 is the 2nd person, masculine, singular pronoun "you", thus 𐤀𐤔𐤏𐤕 means "you will do".

Explanation: "Do' and "make" are equivalents words. Context will help determine how you should translate 𐤀𐤔𐤏𐤕. Due to the presence of the negative participle 𐤀𐤋 (La-Ah), 𐤕𐤏𐤔𐤄 (Tha-I-Sha-Ha) means "you will not do".

Phoenician Hebrew Word: 𐤋𐤊
Transliteration: Ka-La
1611 KJV (AV) | Gloss: any | all-of

Word: 𐤋𐤊 (masculine, singular, noun) means "whole", "all", or "everything" and is indexed to Strong's #3605. Brown-Driver-Brigg's Meanings: all, the whole, the whole of, any, each, every, anything, totality, everything.

Phoenician Hebrew Word: 𐤄𐤊𐤀𐤋𐤌
Transliteration: Ma-La-Ah-Ka-Ha
1611 KJV (AV) | Gloss: work | work

Base Word: 𐤄𐤊𐤀𐤋𐤌 (Ma-La-Ah-Ka-Ha) (feminine, noun) means business and is indexed to Strong's #4399. Brown-Driver-Brigg's Meanings: occupation, business, property, work (something done or made), workmanship, service, use, public business, political, religious.

Phoenician Hebrew Word: 𐤀𐤕𐤄
Transliteration: Ah-Tha-Ha
1611 KJV (AV) | Gloss: thou | you

Word: 𐤀𐤕𐤄 means "you" (2nd person, masculine, singular, pronoun) and is indexed to Strong's #859.

Phoenician Hebrew Word: 𐤊𐤍𐤁𐤅
Transliteration: Wa-Ba-Na-Ka
1611 KJV (AV) | Gloss: nor thy son | or-son-of-you

Base Word: 𐤁𐤍 (Ba-Na) (noun) means "son, grandson, child, member of a group, son, male child, grandson, children (*plural — male and female*), youth, young men (*plural*), young (of animals), sons (as characterisation, i.e. sons of injustice [for unrighteous men] or sons of God [for angels]), people (of a nation), of lifeless things, i.e. sparks, stars, arrows (figuratively), a member of a guild, order, class" and is indexed to Strong's #1121. Brown-Driver-Brigg's Meaning: son, male child, grandson, children (plural — male and female), youth, young men (*plural*), young (of animals), *sons (*as characterisation, i.e. sons of injustice [for unrighteous men] or sons of God [for angels]), people (of a nation) (plural), of lifeless things, i.e. sparks, stars, arrows (figuratively), a member of a guild, order, class."

Prefix: 𐤅 (Wa) is the conjunction "and". Depending on the context, some translators render 𐤅 as "or".

Suffix: 𐤊 (Ka) is the 2nd person, masculine, singular, possessive pronouns "your" and "of you".

Phoenician Hebrew Word: 𐤊𐤕𐤁𐤅
Transliteration: Wa-Ba-Tha-Ka
1611 KJV (AV) | Gloss: nor thy daughter | or-daughter-of-you

Base Word: 𐤕𐤁 (Ba-Tha) (feminine noun) is indexed to Strong's #1323 and means "daughter". Brown-Driver-Brigg's Meanings: daughter, girl, adopted daughter, daughter-in-law, sister, granddaughters, female child, cousin, as polite address, as designation of women of a particular place (noun proper feminine), young women, women (noun feminine), as personification, daughter-villages, description of character.

Prefix: 𐤅 (Wa) is the conjunction "and". Depending on the context, some translators render 𐤅 as "or".

Suffix: 𐤊 (Ka) is the 2nd person, masculine, singular, possessive pronouns "your" and "of you".

Phoenician Hebrew Word: 𐤊𐤃𐤁𐤏
Transliteration: I-Ba-Da-Ka
1611 KJV (AV) | Gloss: nor your manservant | male slave of you

Base Word: 𐤃𐤁𐤏 (I-Ba-Da) (masculine, noun) means "servant" and is indexed to Strong's #5650. Brown-Driver-Brigg's Meanings: slave, servant, slave, servant, man-servant, subjects, servants, worshippers (of God), servant (in a special sense as prophets, Levites etc), servant (of Israel), servant (as form of address between equals).

Suffix: 𐤊 (Ka) is the 2nd person, masculine, singular, possessive pronouns "your" and "of you".

Phoenician Hebrew Word: 𐤊𐤕𐤌𐤀𐤅
Transliteration: Wa-Ah-Ma-Tha-Ka
1611 KJV (AV) | Gloss: nor thou maidservant | or-female-slave-of-you

Base Word: 𐤄𐤌𐤀 (Ah-Ma-Ha) (feminine, noun) means "maid-servant" and is indexed to Strong's #519. Brown-Driver-Brigg's Meanings: maid-servant, female slave, maid, handmaid, concubine.

Prefix: 𐤅 (Wa) is the conjunction "and". Depending on the context, some translators render 𐤅 as "or".

Suffix: 𐤊 (Ka) is the 2nd person, masculine, singular, possessive pronouns "your" and "of you".

Explanation: When two nouns are in the construct state and one of them is feminine whose last pictograph is the 𐤄 (Ha), the 𐤄 must be deleted as shown here 𐤊𐤕𐤌𐤀𐤅 and replaced with the 𐤕 (Tha) which, in this case forms the word 𐤊𐤕𐤌𐤀𐤅.

Phoenician Hebrew Word: 𐤊𐤕𐤌𐤄𐤁𐤅
Transliteration: Wa-Ba-Ha-Ma-Tha-Ka
1611 KJV (AV) | Gloss: nor thy cattle | or-live-livestock-of-you

Base Word: 𐤄𐤌𐤄𐤁 (Ba-Ha-Ma-Ha) (feminine noun) is indexed to Strong's #929 and means "livestock". Brown-Driver-Brigg's Meanings: beast, cattle, animal, livestock, wild beast.

Prefix: 𐤅 (Wa) is the conjunction "and". Depending on the context, some translators render 𐤅 as "or".

Suffix: 𐤊 (Ka) is the 2nd person, masculine, singular, possessive pronouns "your" and "of you".

Explanation: Here is how 𐤊𐤕𐤌𐤄𐤁𐤅 (Wa-Ba-Ha-Ma-Tha-Ka) is constructed:

Step 1: Root word 𐤄𐤌𐤄𐤁 + 𐤅 (Wa) (conjunction) + 𐤊 (Ka) (2nd person, masculine, singular, possessive pronoun)

Step 2: When two nouns are in the construct state and one of them is a feminine noun such as 𐤄𐤌𐤄𐤁 whose last pictograph is the 𐤄 (Ha), the 𐤄 must be deleted and replaced with the 𐤕 (Tha) as shown here 𐤕~~𐤄~~𐤌𐤄𐤁 (Ba-Ha-Ma-~~Ha~~-Tha) which leaves 𐤕𐤌𐤄𐤁 (Ba-Ma-Ha-Tha)

Step 3: The prefix 𐤅 (Wa) (conjunction) + 𐤕𐤌𐤄𐤁 (Ba-Ma-Ha-Tha) from Step 3 + the suffix 𐤊 (Ka) (2nd person, masculine, singular, possessive pronoun) forms the word 𐤊𐤕𐤌𐤄𐤁𐤅 (Wa-Ba-Ha-Ma-Tha-Ka).

Phoenician Hebrew Word: 𐤅𐤂𐤅

Transliteration: Wa-Ga-Ra-Ka
1611 KJV (AV) | Gloss: nor thy stranger | or-sojourner-of-you

Base Word: ꞁꞁ (Ga-Ra) (masculine, noun) means "stranger" and is indexed to Strong's #1616. Brown-Driver-Brigg's Meanings: sojourner, a temporary inhabitant, a newcomer lacking inherited rights, of foreigners in Israel, though conceded rights.

Prefix: ꞁ (Wa) is the conjunction "and". Depending on the context, some translators render ꞁ as "or".

Suffix: ꓺ (Ka) is the 2nd person, masculine, singular, possessive pronoun "your" or "of you".

Phoenician Hebrew Word: ꞁW⚹
Transliteration: Ah-Sha-Ra
1611 KJV (AV) | Gloss: that | who

Word: ꞁW⚹ (Ah-Sha-Ra) (genderless, numberless, relative participle) means "who, what, which, that" and is indexed to Strong's #834. Brown-Driver-Brigg's Meanings: (relative participle) which, who, that which, (conjunction) that (in object clause), when, since, as, conditional if.

Phoenician Hebrew Word: ꓺꓬꞁOWⳆ
Transliteration: Ba-Sha-I-Ra-Ya-Ka
1611 KJV (AV) | Gloss: within thy gates | in-gates-of-you

Base Word: ꞁOW (Sha-I-Ra) (masculine, noun) means "gates" and is indexed to Strong's #8179. Brown-Driver-Brigg's Meanings: gate, gate (of entrance), gate (of space inside gate, i.e. marketplace, public meeting place), city, town, gate (of palace, royal castle, temple, court of tabernacle), heaven.

Prefix: Ⳇ (Ba) is the preposition "in", thus ꞁOW (Sha-I-Ra) means "in the gate".

Suffix: 𝒴𝒵 (Ya-Ma) tells us that ꟻOW (Ba-I-Sha) (noun) is plural, thus 𝒴𝒵ꟻOWᔕ, (Ba-Sha-I-Ra-Ya-Ka) thus "in the gates". The suffix 𝒴 (Ka) is the 2nd person, masculine, singular, possessive pronoun "of you", "your", thus 𝒴𝒵ꟻOWᔕ (Ba-Sha-I-Ra-Ya-Ka) means "in your gates".

Explanation: Here is how 𝒴𝒵ꟻOWᔕ (Ba-Sha-I-Ra-Ya-Ka) is constructed:

Step 1: the root word ꟻOW (Sha-I-Ra) (masculine, noun) + the prefix ᔕ (Ba) (preposition) + the plural suffix 𝒴𝒵 (Ya-Ma) + the suffix 𝒴 (Ka) (2nd person, masculine, singular, possessive pronoun)

Step 2: 𝒴𝒵ꟻOWᔕ (Ba-Sha-I-Ra-Ya-Ka) (noun) is in the construct state. Why? Because when two nouns occur next to each other they are said to be in the construct state. If one of the nouns have the 𝒴𝒵 (Ya-Ma) plural suffix, the 𝒴 (Ma) in the plural suffix 𝒴𝒵 (Ya-Ma) must be deleted as shown here 𝒴 + ~~𝒴~~𝒵 + ꟻOW + ᔕ which forms the word 𝒴𝒵ꟻOWᔕ (Ba-Sha-I-Ra-Ya-Ka).

Write your own literal translation of Exodus 20:10 in the space below:

Ancient: _____

Paleo: _____

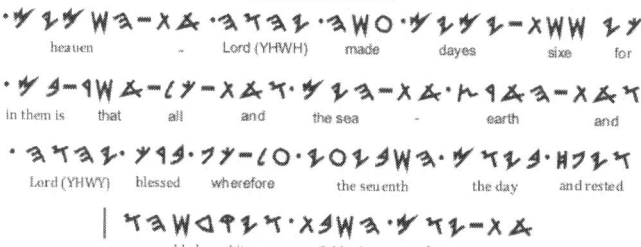

Exodus 20:11

For in sixe dayes the Lord made heauen and earth, the sea, and all that in them is, and rested the seuenth day: wherefore the Lord blessed the Sabbath day, and halowed it.

Phoenician Hebrew Word: 𐤊𐤉
Transliteration: Ka-Ya
1611 KJV (AV) | Gloss: Wherefore | for

Word: 𐤊𐤉 (Ka-Ya) (conjunction) means "because" and is indexed to Strong's #3588. Brown-Driver-Brigg's Meanings: that, for, because, when, as though, as, because that, but, then, certainly, except, surely, since.

Phoenician Hebrew Word: 𐤔𐤔𐤕
Transliteration: Sha-Sha-Tha
1611 KJV (AV) | Gloss: sixe | six of

Word: 𐤔𐤔𐤄 (Sha-Sha-Ha) (adjective) means "six" and is indexed to Strong's #8337. Brown-Driver-Brigg's Meanings: six (*cardinal number*), sixth (*ordinal number*), six in combination with other numbers.

Explanation: The adjective 𐤔𐤔𐤄 (Sha-Sha-Ha) is functioning like a noun in this verse. How do we know? Keep reading if you want to find out!

Here are the rules to determine if an adjective is functioning like a noun:

Rule 1) A Phoenician Hebrew adjective must occur after the noun it describes. In this case, 𐤄𐤔𐤔 (Sha-Sha-Ha) occurs before the noun 𐤌𐤉𐤌𐤉 (Ya-Ma-Ya-Ma) that it describes, so it cannot be an adjective.

Rule 2) The construct state cannot be formed with an adjective. In this case, according to Rule 1 above, 𐤄𐤔𐤔 (Sha-Sha-Ha) is noun and the word that occurs after it is the noun, 𐤌𐤉𐤌𐤉 (Ya-Ma-Ya-Ma), thus the construct state is present.

Rule 3) A Phoenician Hebrew adjective must agree in gender and number with the noun it describes. In this case, 𐤄𐤔𐤔 is singular but the noun 𐤌𐤉𐤌𐤉 it describes is plural, thus 𐤄𐤔𐤔 is functioning as a noun here.

Because the last pictograph in 𐤄𐤔𐤔 is the 𐤄 (Ha), the 𐤄 must be deleted and replaced with 𐤕 (Tha) as shown here (𐤕𐤔𐤔), which this case forms the word 𐤕𐤔𐤔 (Sha-Sha-Tha).

Phoenician Hebrew Word: 𐤌𐤉𐤌𐤉
Transliteration: Ya-Ma-Ya-Ma
1611 KJV (AV) | Gloss: days | days

Base Word: 𐤌𐤅𐤉 (Ya-Wa-Ma) (masculine, noun) means "day", "period of daylight" and is indexed to Strong's #3117. Brown-Driver-Brigg's Meanings: day, time, year, day (as opposed to night), day (24 hour period), as defined by evening and morning in Genesis as a division of time, a working day, a day's journey, days, lifetime, time, period (general), year, temporal references, today, yesterday, tomorrow.

Suffix: 𐤉𐤌 (Ya-Ma) tells us that 𐤉𐤌𐤉𐤌 (Ya-Ma-Ya-Ma) is plural.

Explanation: Here is how the noun 𐤉𐤌𐤉𐤌 is constructed:

Step 1: Root word 𐤉𐤅𐤌 (Ya-Wa-Ma) (noun) + the plural suffix 𐤉𐤌 (Ya-Ma)

Step 2: 𐤉𐤌𐤉𐤌 (Ya-Ma-Ya-Ma) (noun) and 𐤔𐤔𐤕 (Sha-Sha-Tha) (noun) are in the construct state. When two nouns occur next to each other they are said to be in the construct state and the word "of" must be inserted between them when translating them in English, thus 𐤉𐤌𐤉𐤌 * 𐤔𐤔𐤕 means "six of [the] days".

Phoenician Hebrew Word: 𐤏𐤔𐤄
Transliteration: I-Sha-Ha
1611 KJV (AV) | Gloss: he made | he made

Root Word: 𐤏𐤔𐤄 (I-Sha-Ha) (verb) means "do", "make" and is indexed to Strong's #6213. Brown-Driver-Brigg's Meanings: to do, fashion, accomplish, make, work, produce, to deal (with), to act, act with effect, effect, to make, to produce, to prepare, to make (an offering), to attend to, put in order, to observe, celebrate, to acquire (property), to appoint, ordain, institute, to bring about, to use, to spend, pass.

Explanation: 𐤏𐤔𐤄 (I-Sha-Ha) (verb) does not have a prefix or suffix attached to it. This tells us that 𐤏𐤔𐤄 is written in the present tense and the subject of 𐤏𐤔𐤄 is the 3rd person, masculine, singular, pronoun "he", 𐤏𐤔𐤄 means "he did".

Phoenician Hebrew Word: 𐤄𐤅𐤄𐤉
Transliteration: Ya-Ha-Wa-Ha
1611 KJV (AV) | Gloss: Lord | Yahweh

Root Word: 𐤄𐤅𐤄 (Ha-Wa-Ha) (verb) means "to fall out, come to pass, become, be" and is indexed to Strong's #1961. Brown-Driver-Brigg's Meanings: to be, become, come to pass, exist, happen, fall out, [verb form nuances:] to happen, fall out, occur, take place, come about, come to pass, to come about, come to pass, to come into being, become, to arise, appear, come, to become, to become, to become like, to be instituted, be established, to be, to exist, be in existence, to abide, remain, continue (with word of place or time), to stand, lie, be in, be at, be situated (with word of locality), to accompany, be with, to occur, come to pass, be done, be brought about, to be done, be finished, be gone.

Prefix: 𐤉 (Ya) tells us that the subject of the verb 𐤄𐤅𐤄 (Ha-Wa-Ha) is the 3rd person, masculine, singular, pronoun "he", thus 𐤄𐤅𐤄𐤉 means "he exists" or any of the various meanings given above. Of course, context is always helpful to determine a word's meaning and how to render it in English.

Explanation: Jewish people have a tradition of saying "adonai" (Strong's #136) when they read the name 𐤄𐤅𐤄𐤉 (YHWH (YHVH)). The Modern Hebrew vowel pointings in 𐤄𐤅𐤄𐤉 come from the vowel pointings in the word "adonai". The vowels are based on Jewish traditions and have nothing to do with the original pronunciation of 𐤄𐤅𐤄𐤉.

Following the Greek custom, Jewish grammarians combined the present and future tenses of the ancient Phoenician Hebrew Language into one tense (the Imperfect tense). For example, the words Ahayah and YHWH (YHVH) are merely different tenses of the same verb, "hayah" (Strong's #1961). What are the present and future tense conjugations of the verb hayah and what are there meanings? Why is YHWH (YHVH) considered a divine name? There is much more to this topic! Do you want to know more? If yes, Zion Law School will teach you all there is to know, grammatically, about the divines. Visit us online at zionlawschool.org and enroll in the 503 Biblical Hebrew Translations Skills class and the 504 Ten Commandments class. We are looking forward to seeing you in class!

Phoenician Hebrew Word: ×⩜
Transliteration: Ah-Tha
1611 KJV (AV) | Gloss: untranslated

Word: ×⩜ (untranslated, particle, direct object pointer) is indexed to Strong's #853 and is always written before the definite direct object of the last verb. Brown-Driver-Brigg's Meanings: sign of the definite direct object, not translated in English but generally preceding and indicating the accusative.

Phoenician Hebrew Word: ϒʊϒWℨ
Transliteration: Ha-Sha-Ma-Ya-Ma
1611 KJV (AV) | Gloss: heaven | the-heaven

Base Word: ϒʊϒW (Sha-Ma-Ya-Ma) (masculine, noun) is indexed to Strong's #8064 and means "sky". Brown-Driver-Brigg's Meanings: heaven, heavens, sky, visible heavens, sky as abode of the stars, as the visible universe, the sky, atmosphere, etc, Heaven (as the abode of God).

Prefix(es): ℨ (Ha) is the article "the".

Explanation: The last verb in this verse was ℨWO (I-Sha-Ha) which means "do", "make" or "making", thus ℨWO (I-Sha-Ha) (verb) is the "made" in "he made". The subject of the verb ℨWO is the "he" in "he made". The definite direct object of the verb ℨWO is this word ϒʊϒWℨ (Ha-Sha-Ma-Ya-Ma) which means "sky".

Phoenician Hebrew Word: 𐤗𐤀𐤕
Transliteration: Wa-Ah-Tha
1611 KJV (AV) | Gloss: untranslated

Word: 𐤀𐤕 (untranslated, particle, direct object pointer) is indexed at Strong's #853 and always written before the definite direct object of the last verb. Brown-Driver-Brigg's Meanings: sign of the definite direct object, not translated in English but generally preceding and indicating the accusative.

Prefix: 𐤗 (Wa) is the conjunction "and".

Phoenician Hebrew Word: 𐤄𐤀𐤓𐤑
Transliteration: Ha-Ah-Ra-Taza
1611 KJV (AV) | Gloss: earth | the earth

Base Word: 𐤀𐤓𐤑 (Ah-Ra-Taza) (masculine, noun) means "land", "country", "ground", "soil" and is indexed to Strong's #776. means "land" (masculine, noun) and is indexed to Strong's #776. Brown-Driver-Brigg's Meanings: land, whole earth (as opposed to a part), earth (inhabitants), land, country, territory, district, region, tribal territory, piece of ground, land of Canaan, Israel, inhabitants of land, Sheol, land without return, (under) world.

Prefix(es): 𐤄 (Ha) is the article "the".

Explanation: 𐤄𐤀𐤓𐤑 (Ha-Ah-Ra-Taza) is the second definite direct object of the last verb, 𐤑𐤔𐤏 (I-Sha-Ha).

Phoenician Hebrew Word: 𐤀𐤕
Transliteration: Ah-Tha
1611 KJV (AV) | Gloss: untranslated

Word: 𐤀𐤕 (untranslated, particle, direct object pointer) is indexed at Strong's #853 and always written before the definite direct object of the last verb. Brown-Driver-Brigg's Meanings:

sign of the definite direct object, not translated in English but generally preceding and indicating the accusative.

Phoenician Hebrew Word: 𐤌𐤉𐤄
Transliteration: Ha-Ya-Ma
1611 KJV (AV) | Gloss: the sea | the-sea

Base Word: 𐤌𐤉 (Ya-Ma) (masculine, noun) means "sea" and is indexed to Strong's #3220. Brown-Driver-Brigg's Meanings: sea (Mediterranean Sea, Red Sea, Dead, Sea, Sea of Galilee, sea (general), mighty river (Nile), the sea (the great basin in the temple court), seaward, west, westward.

Prefix: 𐤄 (Ha) is the article "the", thus means "the sea".

Explanation: 𐤌𐤉𐤄 (Ha-Ya-Ma) is the third definite direct object of the last verb, 𐤄𐤔𐤏 (I-Sha-Ha).

Phoenician Hebrew Word: 𐤕𐤀𐤅
Transliteration: Wa-Ah-Tha
1611 KJV (AV) | Gloss: untranslated

Word: 𐤕𐤀 (untranslated, particle, direct object pointer) is indexed at Strong's #853 and always written before the definite direct object of the last verb. Brown-Driver-Brigg's Meanings: sign of the definite direct object, not translated in English but generally preceding and indicating the accusative.

Prefix: 𐤅 (Wa) is the conjunction "and".

Phoenician Hebrew Word: 𐤋𐤊
Transliteration: Ka-La
1611 KJV (AV) | Gloss: all | all-of

Word 𐤋𐤊 (masculine, singular, noun) means "any, all, complete, every" and is indexed to Strong's #3605. Brown-

Driver-Brigg's Meanings: all, the whole, the whole of, any, each, every, anything, totality, everything.

Phoenician Hebrew Word: ꍏW꒜
Transliteration: Ah-Sha-Ra
1611 KJV (AV) | Gloss: that | that

Word: ꍏW꒜ (Ah-Sha-Ra) (genderless, numberless, relative participle) means "who, what, which, that" and is indexed to Strong's #834. Brown-Driver-Brigg's Meanings: (relative participle) which, who, that which, (conjunction) that (in object clause), when, since, as, conditional if.

Phoenician Hebrew Word: ꓩꝞ
Transliteration: Ba-Ma
1611 KJV (AV) | Gloss: in them is | in them
Word: No base word. No Strong's #.

Prefix: ꓩ (Ba) is the preposition "in".

Suffix: Ꝟ (Ma) is the 3rd person, masculine, plural, pronoun "them".

Explanation: The last four words of this verse form the phrase ꓩꝞ(Ba-Ma)*ꍏW꒜(Ah-Sha-Ra)*ꝈꝞ(Ka-La)*ꓩ꒜ꓕ(Wa-Ah-Tha) which means "all which are in them" which is the fourth definite direct object of the last verb, ꓱWO (I-Sha-Ha).

Phoenician Hebrew Word: ꓧꓩꝞꓕ
Transliteration: Wa-Ya-Na-Chaa
1611 KJV (AV) | Gloss: and rested | and-he-rested

Root Word: ꓧꓕꓩ (Na-Wa-Chaa) (verb) means "rest" and is indexed to Strong's #5117.

Prefix: ꓕ (Wa) is the conjunction "and". Ꝟ (Ya) tells us that the root word 𐤇𐤅𐤍 (Na-Wa-Chaa) (verb) is written in the imperfect tense, "will rest". 𐤉 (Ya) also tells us that the subject of the verb 𐤇𐤅𐤍 (Na-Wa-Chaa) is the third person, masculine, singular, pronoun "he", thus 𐤅𐤉𐤍𐤇 (Wa-Ya-Na-Chaa) means "he will rest". 𐤅 (Wa) also reverses the tense of the verb 𐤅𐤉𐤍𐤇 (Wa-Ya-Na-Chaa) to "and he rested". 𐤅𐤉𐤍𐤇 is rendered "and rested" in the 1611 KJV (AV).

Explanation: Here is how the word 𐤅𐤉𐤍𐤇 is constructed:

Step 1: When conjugating this verb 𐤇𐤅𐤍 (Na-Wa-Chaa), the 𐤅 (Wa) is deleted as shown here 𐤇̶𐤅̶𐤍 (Na-W̶a̶-Chaa).

Step 2: Root word 𐤍𐤇 (Na-Chaa) (verb) + the prefix 𐤉 (Ya) (3rd person, masculine, singular, pronoun) + the prefix 𐤅 (Wa) (conjunction) (reverse Wa) which forms the word 𐤅𐤉𐤍𐤇.

Phoenician Hebrew Word: 𐤁𐤉𐤅𐤌
Transliteration: Ba-Ya-Wa-Ma
1611 KJV (AV) | Gloss: in the day | on-the-day

Base Word: 𐤌𐤅𐤉 (Ya-Wa-Ma) (masculine, noun) means "day", "period of daylight" and is indexed to Strong's #3117. Brown-Driver-Brigg's Meanings: day, time, year, day (as opposed to night), day (24 hour period), as defined by evening and morning in Genesis as a division of time, a working day, a day's journey, days, lifetime, time, period (general), year, temporal references, today, yesterday, tomorrow.

Prefix: 𐤁 (Ba) is the preposition "in".

Phoenician Hebrew Word: 𐤄𐤔𐤁𐤉𐤏𐤉
Transliteration: Ha-Sha-Ba-Ya-I-Ya
1611 KJV (AV) | Gloss: the seventh | the seventh
Base Word: 𐤔𐤁𐤉𐤏𐤉 (Sha-Ba-Ya-I-Ya) (adjective) means "seventh" and is indexed to Strong's #7637.
Prefix: 𐤄 (Ha) is the article "the".
Explanation: The adverb 𐤄𐤔𐤁𐤉𐤏𐤉 (Ha-Sha-Ba-Ya-I-Ya) describes the noun 𐤁𐤉𐤅𐤌 (Ba-Ya-Wa-Ma) that occurred immediately before it and means, "in day". 𐤁𐤉𐤅𐤌 * 𐤄𐤔𐤁𐤉𐤏𐤉 forms the phrase "in [the] day the seventh". To make this phrase easier to understand some translators render it "on the seventh day" and the 1611 KJV (AV) renders it "the seventh day"

Phoenician Hebrew Word: 𐤏𐤋
Transliteration: I-La
1611 KJV (AV) | Gloss: not rendered | upon
Word: 𐤏𐤋 is a preposition indexed to Strong's #5921 and means "upon". Brown-Driver-Brigg's Meanings: "upon, on the ground of, according to, on account of, on behalf of, concerning, beside, in addition to, together with, beyond, above, over, by, on to, towards, to, against (preposition), down upon, upon, on, from, up upon, up to, towards, over towards, to, against (with verbs of motion).

Phoenician Hebrew Word: 𐤊𐤍
Transliteration: Ka-Na
1611 KJV (AV) | Gloss: wherefore | thus
Word: 𐤊𐤍 (Ka-Na) (adverb) means "so" and is indexed to Strong's #3651.

Explanation: The word immediately before this word 𐤊𐤍 (Ka-Na) is 𐤏𐤋 (I-La), which means "upon". These two words are combined to render them as "therefore".

Phoenician Hebrew Word: 𐤊𐤓𐤁
Transliteration: Ba-Ra-Ka
1611 KJV (AV) | Gloss: blessed | he blessed

Root Word: 𐤊𐤓𐤁 (Ba-Ra-Ka) (verb) is indexed to Strong's #1288 and has several meanings. In its passive form, 𐤊𐤓𐤁 (Ba-Ra-Ka) means "to kneel". In its intensive and active form, 𐤊𐤓𐤁 (Ba-Ra-Ka) means "to bless The Most High as in an act of adoration" or "to bless man with a benefit". Alternatively, 𐤊𐤓𐤁 (Ba-Ra-Ka) is used as a mild or indirect word that is substituted for a word that is considered to be too harsh or blunt when referring to something unpleasant or embarrassing. For example, 𐤊𐤓𐤁 (Ba-Ra-Ka) also means "to curse The Most High" and "to curse the king (as in treason)". Brown-Driver-Brigg's Meanings: to bless, kneel; [verb form nuances:] to kneel, to be blessed, bless oneself, be adored, to cause to kneel, (*TWOT*) to praise, salute, curse.

Explanation: 𐤊𐤓𐤁 (Ba-Ra-Ka) (verb) does not have a prefix or suffix attached to it. This fact tells us that 𐤊𐤓𐤁 is written in the perfect tense and that the subject of 𐤊𐤓𐤁 is the 3rd person, masculine, singular, pronoun "he", thus, 𐤊𐤓𐤁 is rendered "he halowed".

Phoenician Hebrew Word: 𐤄𐤅𐤄𐤉
Transliteration: Ya-Ha-Wa-Ha
1611 KJV (AV) | Gloss: Lord | Yahweh

Root Word: 𐤄𐤅𐤄 (Ha-Wa-Ha) (verb) means "to fall out, come to pass, become, be" and is indexed to Strong's #1961.

Brown-Driver-Brigg's Meanings: to be, become, come to pass, exist, happen, fall out, [verb form nuances:] to happen, fall out, occur, take place, come about, come to pass, to come about, come to pass, to come into being, become, to arise, appear, come, to become, to become, to become like, to be instituted, be established, to be, to exist, be in existence, to abide, remain, continue (with word of place or time), to stand, lie, be in, be at, be situated (with word of locality), to accompany, be with, to occur, come to pass, be done, be brought about, to be done, be finished, be gone.

Prefix: 𐤉 (Ya) tells us that the subject of the verb 𐤄𐤅𐤄 (Ha-Wa-Ha) is the 3rd person, masculine, singular, pronoun "he", thus 𐤄𐤅𐤄𐤉 means "he exists" or any of the various meanings given above. Of course, context is always helpful to determine a word's meaning and how to render it in English.

Explanation: Jewish people have a tradition of saying "adonai" (Strong's #136) when they read the name 𐤄𐤅𐤄𐤉 (YHWH (YHVH)). The Modern Hebrew vowel pointings in 𐤄𐤅𐤄𐤉 come from the vowel pointings in the word "adonai". The vowels are based on Jewish traditions and have nothing to do with the original pronunciation of 𐤄𐤅𐤄𐤉.

Following the Greek custom, Jewish grammarians combined the present and future tenses of the ancient Phoenician Hebrew Language into one tense (the Imperfect tense). For example, the words Ahayah and YHWH (YHVH) are merely different tenses of the same verb, "hayah" (Strong's #1961). What are the present and future tense conjugations of the verb hayah and what are there meanings? Why is YHWH (YHVH) considered a divine name? There is much more to this topic! Do you want to know more? If yes, Zion Law School will teach you all there is to know, grammatically, about the divines. Visit us online at zionlawschool.org and enroll in the 503 Biblical Hebrew Translations Skills class and the 504 Ten Commandments class. We are looking forward to seeing you in class!

Phoenician Hebrew Word: 𐤀𐤕
Transliteration: Ah-Tha
1611 KJV (AV) | Gloss: untranslated

Word: 𐤀𐤕 (untranslated, particle, direct object pointer) is indexed at Strong's #853 and is always written before the definite direct object of the last verb. Brown-Driver-Brigg's Meanings: sign of the definite direct object, not translated in English but generally preceding and indicating the accusative.

Phoenician Hebrew Word: 𐤉𐤅𐤌
Transliteration: Ya-Wa-Ma
1611 KJV (AV) | Gloss: day | day-of

Base Word: 𐤉𐤅𐤌 (Ya-Wa-Ma) (masculine, noun) is indexed to Strong's #3117 and means "day", "period of daylight". Brown-Driver-Brigg's Meanings: day, time, year, day (as opposed to night), day (24 hour period), as defined by evening and morning in Genesis as a division of time, a working day, a day's journey, days, lifetime, time, period (general), year, temporal references, today, yesterday, tomorrow.

Phoenician Hebrew Word: 𐤄𐤔𐤁𐤕
Transliteration: Ha-Sha-Ba-Tha
1611 KJV (AV) | Gloss: Sabbath | the Sabbath

Base Word: 𐤔𐤁𐤕 (Sha-Ba-Tha) (noun) means "intermission, desist from exertion" is indexed to Strong's #7676. Brown-Driver-Brigg's Meanings: Sabbath, sabbath, day of, atonement, sabbath year, week, produce (in sabbath year).

Prefix: 𐤄 (Ha) is the article "the".

Explanation: The word 𐤄𐤔𐤁𐤕 (Ha-Sha-Ba-Tha) (noun) and 𐤉𐤅𐤌 (Ya-Wa-Ma) (noun) are in the construct state, therefore, to render the phrase 𐤄𐤔𐤁𐤕 * 𐤉𐤅𐤌 in English the word "of" must be inserted between them, which forms the phrase "day of the Sabbath". To make this phrase easier to understand, the article "the" is moved from in front of "the Sabbath" and placed it in front of the word "day" to yield "the day of Shabbat". The 1611 KJV (AV) renders this phrase as "Sabbath day".

Phoenician Hebrew Word: ᚼᚴᚹ◁ᚹᛉᚼ
Transliteration: Wa-Ya-Qa-Da-Sha-Ha-Wa
1611 KJV (AV) | Gloss: and hallowed it | and-he-made-holy-him

Root Word: ᚹ◁ᚹ (Qa-Da-Sha) (verb) means "appoint, bid, consecrate, dedicate, defile, hallow (halow), be holy," and is indexed to Strong's #6942. Brown-Driver-Brigg's Meanings: to consecrate, sanctify, prepare, dedicate, be hallowed, be holy, be sanctified, be separate, [verb form nuances:] to be set apart, be consecrated, tabooed.

Prefix: ᛉ (Ya) tells us that ᚹ◁ᚹ (Qa-Da-Sha) is written in the imperfect tense, thus ᚹ◁ᚹ (Qa-Da-Sha) means "will hallow". ᛉ (Ya) also tells us that the subject of ᚹ◁ᚹ is the 3rd person, masculine, singular, pronoun "he", thus ᚹ◁ᚹᛉ means "he will hallow".

ᚼ (Wa) is the conjunction "and". ᚼ (Wa) also reverses the tense of ᚹ◁ᚹᛉ (Ya-Qa-Da-Sha) to perfect tense, thus ᚹ◁ᚹᛉᚼ (Wa-Ya-Qa-Da-Sha) means "and he hallowed".

Suffix: ᚼᚴ (Ha-Wa) tells us that the object of ᚹ◁ᚹᛉᚼ is the 3rd person, masculine, singular, pronoun "him", thus ᚼᚴᚹ◁ᚹᛉᚼ (Wa-Ya-Qa-Da-Sha-Ha-Wa) means "and he hallowed him". The 1611 KJV (AV) renders ᚼᚴᚹ◁ᚹᛉᚼ (Wa-Ya-Qa-Da-Sha-Ha-Wa) as "and hallowed it".

Explanation: The subject of the verb ᚹ◁ᚹ (Qa-Da-Sha) is

the "he" in "and he hallowed him" and refers to the name 𐤉𐤄𐤅𐤄 (YHWH (YHVH)) that occurred earlier in this verse. The object of the verb 𐤒𐤃𐤔 (Qa-Da-Sha) is the "him" in "and he hallowed him" and refers to the noun 𐤉𐤅𐤌 (Ya-Wa-Ma), which means "day", that occurred earlier in this verse.

Write your own literal translation of Exodus 20:11 in the space below:

<u>Ancient Script</u>: _____
_____
_____
_____

<u>Paleo Script</u>: _____
_____
_____
_____

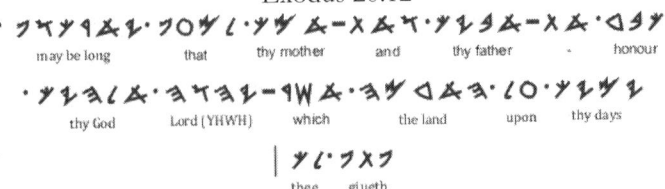

Exodus 20:12

Honour thy father and thy mother: that thy dayes may bee long vpon the land, which the Lord thy God giueth thee.

Phoenician Hebrew Word: ᐊᒡᵞ
Transliteration: Ka-Ba-Da
1611 KJV (AV) | Gloss: honour | honor

Base Word: ᐊᒡᵞ (Ka-Ba-Da) (verb) means "be heavy, weighty, burdensome, honoured, be hard, be rich" and is indexed to Strong's #3513. Brown-Driver-Brigg's Meanings: to be heavy, be weighty, be grievous, be hard, be rich, be honourable, be glorious, be burdensome, be honoured; [verb form nuances:] to be heavy, be insensible, be dull, to be honoured, to be made heavy, be honoured, enjoy honour, be made abundant, to get oneself glory or honour, gain glory, to make heavy, make dull, make insensible, to make honourable, honour, glorify, to be made honourable, be honoured, to make heavy, make dull, make unresponsive, to cause to be honoured, to make oneself heavy, make oneself dense, make oneself numerous, to honour oneself.

Explanation: In this verse, ᐊᒡᵞ (Ka-Ba-Da) expresses a command in the active voice, thus ᐊᒡᵞ is a command to "give heavy weight or serious consideration to your father and mother in all matters that are lawful".

Phoenician Hebrew Word: ×⫪
Transliteration: Ah-Tha

1611 KJV (AV) | Gloss: untranslated

Word: 𐤀𐤕 (untranslated, particle, direct object pointer) is indexed at Strong's #853 and is always written before the definite direct object of the last verb. Brown-Driver-Brigg's Meanings: sign of the definite direct object, not translated in English but generally preceding and indicating the accusative.

Phoenician Hebrew Word: 𐤀𐤁𐤉𐤊
Transliteration: Ah-Ba-Ya-Ka
1611 KJV (AV) | Gloss: thy father | father-of-you

Base Word: 𐤀𐤁 (Ah-Ba) (masculine, noun) is indexed to Strong's #1 and means "father". Brown-Driver-Brigg's Meanings: father of an individual, of God as father of his people, 3) head or founder of a household, group, family, or clan, ancestor, grandfather, forefathers — of person, of people, originator or, patron of a class, profession, or art (of producer, generator (figuratively), of benevolence and protection (figuratively), term of respect and honour, ruler or chief (specifically).

Suffix: 𐤉 (Ya) is a rare suffix and its presence tells us that 𐤀𐤁𐤉𐤊 (Ah-Ba-Ya-Ka) is in a modified form. 𐤊 (Ka) is the 2nd person, masculine, singular, pronoun "of you" or "your", thus 𐤀𐤁𐤉𐤊 means "father of you", thy father, "your father".

Explanation: 𐤀𐤁𐤉𐤊 (Ah-Ba-Ya-Ka) is the definite direct object of the verb 𐤊𐤁𐤃 (Ka-Ba-Da) which occurs immediately before 𐤀𐤁𐤉𐤊 (Ah-Ba-Ya-Ka).

Phoenician Hebrew Word: 𐤅𐤀𐤕
Transliteration: Wa-Ah-Tha
1611 KJV (AV) | Gloss: and | and—

Word: 𐤀𐤕 (untranslated, particle, direct object pointer) is indexed at Strong's #853 and is always written before the definite direct object of the last verb. Brown-Driver-Brigg's Meanings: sign of the definite direct object, not translated in English but generally preceding and indicating the accusative.

Prefix: 𐤅 (Wa) is the conjunction "and".

Phoenician Hebrew Word: 𐤀𐤌𐤊
Transliteration: Ah-Ma-Ka
1611 KJV (AV) | Gloss: thy mother | mother-of-you

Base Word: 𐤀𐤌 (Ah-Ma) (feminine, noun) means "a mother (as the bond of the family); in a wide sense (both literally and figuratively [like father (chief, principal)], dam, mother, parting." and is indexed to Strong's #517. Brown-Driver-Brigg's Meanings: mother (of humans, of Deborah's relationship to the people (figuratively), of animals), point of departure or division.

Suffix: 𐤊 is the 2nd person, masculine, singular, possessive pronoun "of you" or "your".

Explanation: 𐤀𐤌𐤊 (Ah-Ma-Ka) is the second definite direct object of the verb 𐤊𐤁𐤃 (Ka-Ba-Da), which occured immediately before 𐤀𐤌𐤊.

Phoenician Hebrew Word: 𐤋𐤌𐤏𐤍
Transliteration: La-Ma-I-Na
1611 KJV (AV) | Gloss: that | so that

Base Word: 𐤋𐤌𐤏𐤅 (La-Ma-I-Wa) (preposition) means "because of, to the end intent that, for to," and is indexed to Strong's #4616. Brown-Driver-Brigg's Meanings: purpose, intent, for the sake of (in view of, on account of, for the purpose of, to the intent that, in order to conjunction, to the end that).

Phoenician Hebrew Word: 𐤍𐤅𐤊𐤓𐤀𐤉
Transliteration: Ya-Ah-Ra-Ka-Wa-Na
1611 KJV (AV) | Gloss: may be long | they-will-be-long

Root Word: 𐤊𐤓𐤀 (Ah-Ra-Ka) (verb) means "to be (or make) long (literally or figuratively) -- defer, draw out, lengthen, (be, become, make, prolong, outlive, over live, live, tarry (long)" and is indexed to Strong's #748. Brown-Driver-Brigg's Meanings: to be long, prolong (to be long, to prolong (days), to make long (tent cords), to grow long, continue long).

Prefix: 𐤉 (Ya) tells us that the verb 𐤊𐤓𐤀 is written in the imperfect tense, "will be long".

Suffix: 𐤅 (Wa) tells us that the verb 𐤅𐤊𐤓𐤀 (Ya-Ah-Ra-Ka) is written in the imperfect tense, "will be long" and that the subject of 𐤅𐤊𐤓𐤀 (Ya-Ah-Ra-Ka) is the 3rd person, masculine, plural, pronoun "they", thus 𐤅𐤊𐤓𐤀𐤉 means "they will belong". The suffix 𐤍 (Na) adds an additional emphasis and/or some change in sense. (See explanation below).

Explanation: Our ancient ancestors (scribes) or Jewish editors added the suffix 𐤍 (Na) to original words to add extra or additional emphasis and/or some change in sense of the word. In the case of the original word 𐤅𐤊𐤓𐤀𐤉, the suffix 𐤍 (Na) adds the additional emphasis of "definiteness", "certainty" or "must", thus 𐤍𐤅𐤊𐤓𐤀𐤉 means "they will definitely be long".

Phoenician Hebrew Word: 𐤉𐤊𐤌𐤉
Transliteration: Ya-Ma-Ya-Ka
1611 KJV (AV) | Gloss: thy days | days-of-you

Base Word: 𐤌𐤅𐤉 (Ya-Wa-Ma) (masculine, noun) means "day", "period of daylight" and is indexed to Strong's #3117. Brown-Driver-Brigg's Meanings: day, time, year, day (*as opposed to night*), day (*24 hour period*), as defined by evening and morning in Genesis as a division of time, a working day, a day's journey, days, lifetime, time, period (*general*), year, temporal references, today, yesterday, tomorrow.

Suffix: 𝅘𝅥 𝅘𝅥 (Ya-Ma) tells us that the noun 𝅘𝅥 𝅘𝅥 𝅘𝅥 (Ya-Wa-Ma) is plural, "days". (See explanation below).

𝅘𝅥 (Ka) is the second person, masculine, singular possessive pronoun "of you", "your" and "thy", thus 𝅘𝅥 𝅘𝅥 𝅘𝅥 𝅘𝅥 𝅘𝅥 means "your days", "days of you", "thy days". (See explanation below).
Explanation: When nouns appear with a suffix, they are in their modified state. When the plural suffix 𝅘𝅥 𝅘𝅥 (Ya-Wa-Ma) attached to a noun, the 𝅘𝅥 in 𝅘𝅥 𝅘𝅥 (Ya-Ma) must be deleted as shown here 𝅘𝅥 𝅘𝅥 𝅘𝅥 𝅘𝅥 (Ya-Ma-Ya-Ka), which forms the word 𝅘𝅥 𝅘𝅥 𝅘𝅥 𝅘𝅥.

Phoenician Hebrew Word: 𐤋𐤏
Transliteration: I-La
1611 KJV (AV) | Gloss: upon | on

Word: 𐤋𐤏 is a preposition indexed to Strong's #5921 and means "upon". Brown-Driver-Brigg's Meanings: "upon, on the ground of, according to, on account of, on behalf of, concerning, beside, in addition to, together with, beyond, above, over, by, on to, towards, to, against (preposition), down upon, upon, on, from, up upon, up to, towards, over towards, against (with verbs of motion).

Phoenician Hebrew Word: 𐤄𐤌𐤃𐤀𐤄
Transliteration: Ha-Ah-Da-Ma-Ha
1611 KJV (AV) | Gloss: the land, the-land

Base Word: 𐤄𐤌𐤃𐤀𐤄 (Ha-Ah-Da-Ma-Ha) (feminine, noun)

means "soil (from its general redness) -- country, earth, ground, husband(-man) (-ry), land." and is indexed to Strong's #127 and means "ground". Brown-Driver-Brigg's Meanings: ground, land (ground - as general, tilled, yielding sustenance), piece of ground, a specific plot of land, earth substance (for building or constructing), ground as earth's visible surface, land, territory, country, whole inhabited earth, city in Naphtali)".

Prefix: ᚦ (Ha) is the article "the".

Phoenician Hebrew Word: ᚦWᚦ
Transliteration: Ah-Sha-Ra
1611 KJV (AV) | Gloss: Which | that

Word: ᚦWᚦ (Ah-Sha-Ra) (genderless, numberless, relative participle) means "who, what, which, that" and is indexed to Strong's #834. Brown-Driver-Brigg's Meanings: (relative participle) which, who, that which, (conjunction) that (in object clause), when, since, as, conditional if.

Phoenician Hebrew Word: ᚦYᚦᛉ
Transliteration: Ya-Ha-Wa-Ha
1611 KJV (AV) | Gloss: Lord | Yahweh

Root Word: ᚦYᚦ (Ha-Wa-Ha) (verb) means "to fall out, come to pass, become, be" and is indexed to Strong's #1961. Brown-Driver-Brigg's Meanings: to be, become, come to pass, exist, happen, fall out, [verb form nuances:] to happen, fall out, occur, take place, come about, come to pass, to come about, come to pass, to come into being, become, to arise, appear, come, to become, to become, to become like, to be instituted, be established, to be, to exist, be in existence, to abide, remain, continue (with word of place or time), to stand, lie, be in, be at, be situated (with word of locality), to accompany, be with, to occur, come to pass, be done, be brought about, to be done, be finished, be gone.

Prefix: 𐤉 (Ya) tells us that the subject of the verb 𐤄𐤅𐤄 (Ha-Wa-Ha) is the 3rd person, masculine, singular, pronoun "he", thus 𐤉𐤄𐤅𐤄 means "he exists" or any of the various meanings given above. Of course, context is always helpful to determine a word's meaning and how to render it in English.

Explanation: Jewish people have a tradition of saying "adonai" (Strong's #136) when they read the name 𐤉𐤄𐤅𐤄 (YHWH (YHVH)). The Modern Hebrew vowel pointings in 𐤉𐤄𐤅𐤄 come from the vowel pointings in the word "adonai". The vowels are based on Jewish traditions and have nothing to do with the original pronunciation of 𐤉𐤄𐤅𐤄.

Following the Greek custom, Jewish grammarians combined the present and future tenses of the ancient Phoenician Hebrew Language into one tense (the Imperfect tense). For example, the words Ahayah and YHWH (YHVH) are merely different tenses of the same verb, "hayah" (Strong's #1961). What are the present and future tense conjugations of the verb hayah and what are there meanings? Why is YHWH (YHVH) considered a divine name? There is much more to this topic! Do you want to know more? If yes, Zion Law School will teach you all there is to know, grammatically, about the divines. Visit us online at zionlawschool.org and enroll in the 503 Biblical Hebrew Translations Skills class and the 504 Ten Commandments class. We are looking forward to seeing you in class!

Phoenician Hebrew Word: 𐤊𐤉𐤄𐤋𐤀
Transliteration: Ah-La-Ha-Ya-Ka
1611 KJV (AV) | Gloss: thy God | God-of-you

Base Word: 𐤄𐤅𐤋𐤀 (Ah-La-Wa-Ha) (noun) (shortened spelling 𐤄𐤋𐤀) means a deity, or the Deity and is indexed to Strong's #433. 𐤄𐤅𐤋𐤀 is perhaps the singular form of

𐤌𐤉𐤄𐤋𐤀 (Ah-La-Ha-Ya-Ma) (Strong's #430) and means "gods in the ordinary sense; [plural or with the article] the supreme God; [plural refers to:] human or divine rulers, judges, magistrates, representatives at sacred places or as reflecting divine majesty or power, super human beings such as God and angels; the sons of God or the sons of god = angels; god, goddess".

𐤄𐤋𐤀 is a Hebrew name for "God" that corresponds to the Aramaic elahh (Strong's #426). The origin of the term is unknown. 𐤄𐤋𐤀 is a divine name in the Book of Job but it is rarely used as such in other Bible books. Brown-Driver-Brigg's: rulers, judges, divine ones, angels, gods, god, goddess, godlike one, works or special possessions of God, the (*true*) God, God.

Suffix(es): 𐤌𐤉 (Ya-Ma) tells us that the gender of 𐤄𐤋𐤀 (shortened spelling of 𐤄𐤅𐤋𐤀) is masculine and its number is plural.

𐤌 (Ka) is the 2nd person, masculine, singular possessive pronoun "[of] you", "your".

Explanation: Here is how this word is constructed:

Step 1: Base word 𐤄𐤋𐤀 (Ah-La-Ha) (noun) + plural suffix 𐤌𐤉 (Ya-Ma) + suffix 𐤌 (Ka) (2nd person, masculine, singular possessive pronoun)

Step 2: Because 𐤌𐤉𐤄𐤋𐤀 is in the construct state, the 𐤌 in 𐤌𐤌 (Ya-Ma) must be deleted as shown here 𐤌 + ~~𐤌~~𐤉 + 𐤄𐤋𐤀 which leaves 𐤌 + 𐤉 + 𐤄𐤋𐤀 (Ah-La-Ha-Ya-Ka) to form the word 𐤌𐤉𐤄𐤋𐤀.

Context always determines if the word 𐤌𐤉𐤄𐤋𐤀 (Ah-La-Ha-

Ya-Ka) (noun) is singular or plural. 𐤉𐤌𐤄𐤋𐤀 describes 𐤄𐤅𐤄𐤉 (YHWH (YHVH)) which is singular, therefore, the noun 𐤉𐤌𐤄𐤋𐤀 is also singular.

Phoenician Hebrew Word: 𐤍𐤕𐤍
Transliteration: Na-Tha-Na
1611 KJV (AV) | Gloss: giveth | giving

Verb: 𐤅𐤕𐤍 (Na-Tha-Wa) (verb, particle form) means "add, apply, appoint, ascribe, assign, avenge, be healed, bestow," and is indexed to Strong's #5414. Brown-Driver-Brigg's Meanings: to give, put, set; [verb form nuances:] to give, bestow, grant, permit, ascribe, employ, devote, consecrate, dedicate, pay wages, sell, exchange, lend, commit, entrust, give over, deliver up, yield produce, occasion, produce, requite to, report, mention, utter, stretch out, extend, to put, set, put on, put upon, set, appoint, assign, designate, to make, constitute, to be given, be bestowed, be provided, be entrusted to, be granted to, be permitted, be issued, be published, be uttered, be assigned, to be set, be put, be made, be inflicted, to be given, be bestowed, be given up, be delivered up, to be put upon.

Phoenician Hebrew Word: 𐤋𐤊
Transliteration: La-Ka
1611 KJV (AV) | Gloss: thee | to-you
Word: No base word. No Strong's #.

Prefix: 𐤋 (La) is the preposition "to".

Suffix: 𐤊 (Ka) is the 2nd person, masculine, singular, pronoun "you", thus 𐤋𐤊 (Ka-La) means "to you" or "to thee".

Write your own literal translation of Exodus 20:12 in the space below:

Ancient Script: _____
_____
_____
_____

Paleo Script:_____
_____
_____
_____
_____

Exodus 20:13

| 𐤇𐤓𐤑𐤕 · 𐤀𐤋
thou shalt kill   not

Thou shalt not kill.

Phoenician Hebrew Word: 𐤀𐤋
Transliteration: La-Ah
1611 KJV (AV) | Gloss: not | not

Word: 𐤀𐤋 (negative participle) means "not" and is indexed to Strong's #3808. Brown-Driver-Brigg's Meanings: not, no, not (with verb — absolute prohibition), not (with modifier — negation), nothing (substantive), without (with particle), before (of time).

Explanation: 𐤀𐤋 negates the action of the verb that comes immediately after it. Stated another way, 𐤀𐤋 negates the action of the verb it is associated with.

Phoenician Hebrew Word: 𐤇𐤓𐤑𐤕
Transliteration: Tha-Ra-Taza-Chaa
1611 KJV (AV) | Gloss: thou shalt kill | you-shall-murder

Verb: 𐤇𐤓𐤑 (Ra-Taza-Chaa) (verb) means "murder" and is indexed to Strong's #7523. Brown-Driver-Brigg's Meanings: to murder, slay, kill; [verb form nuances:] to murder, slay, premeditated, accidental, as avenger slayer (intentional) (participle), to be slain, to murder, assassinate, murderer, assassin (participle) (substantive), to be killed.

Prefix: 𐤕 (Tha) tells us that the verb 𐤇𐤓𐤑 (Ra-Taza-Chaa) is written in the imperfect tense, thus 𐤇𐤓𐤑 means "will murder". 𐤕 also tells us that the subject of 𐤓𐤑𐤕 is the 2nd person, masculine, singular, pronoun "you", thus 𐤇𐤓𐤑𐤕 means "you will murder".

Explanation: Recall that when the negative participle 𐤀𐤋 (La-Ah) occurs before a verb, it negates the action of that verb, thus 𐤇𐤓𐤑𐤕 is rendered, "you will not murder".

Write your own literal translation of Exodus 20:13 in the space below:

Ancient Script: _____
_____
_____
_____

Paleo Script: _____
_____
_____
_____

Exodus 20:14

| 𝟏𝄒𝟕𝐗 · 𝄒𝑙
thou shalt commit adultery   not

Thou shalt not commit adultery.

Phoenician Hebrew Word: 𝄒𝑙
Transliteration: La-Ah
1611 KJV (AV) | Gloss: not | not

Word: 𝄒𝑙 (negative participle) means "not" and is indexed to Strong's #3808. Brown-Driver-Brigg's Meanings: not, no, not (with verb — absolute prohibition), not (with modifier — negation), nothing (substantive), without (with particle), before (of time).

Explanation: 𝄒𝑙 negates the action of the verb that comes immediately after it. Stated another way, 𝄒𝑙 negates the action of the verb it is associated with.

Phoenician Hebrew Word: 𝟏𝄒𝟕𝐗
Transliteration: Tha-Na-Ah-Pa
1611 KJV (AV) | Gloss: thou shalt commit adultery | you-shall-commit-adultery

Verb: 𝟏𝄒𝟕 (Na-Ah-Pa) (verb) means "commit adultery" and is indexed to Strong's #5003. Brown-Driver-Brigg's Meanings: to commit adultery; [verb form nuances:] to commit adultery, usually of man, always with wife of another, adultery (of women) (participle), idolatrous worship (figuratively).

Prefix: 𝐗 (Tha) tells us that 𝟏𝄒𝟕 (Na-Ah-Pa) is written in the imperfect tense, "will commit adultery". 𝐗 also tells us that the subject of 𝟏𝄒𝟕 (Na-Ah-Pa) is the 2nd person, masculine, singular, pronoun "you", thus 𝟏𝄒𝟕𝐗 means "you will commit adultery".

Explanation: Recall that when the negative participle 𐤀𐤋 (La-Ah) occurs before a verb, it negates the action of that verb, thus 𐤕𐤀𐤍 means "you will not commit adultery".

Write your own literal translation of Exodus 20:14 in the space below:

Ancient Script: _____
_____
_____
_____

Paleo Script: _____
_____
_____
_____
_____

Exodus 20:15

𐤁𐤍𐤂𐤕 · 𐤀𐤋
thou shalt steal   not

Thou shalt not commit adultery.

Phoenician Hebrew Word: 𐤀𐤋
Transliteration: La-Ah
1611 KJV (AV) | Gloss: not | not

Word: 𐤀𐤋 (negative participle) means "not" and is indexed to Strong's #3808. Brown-Driver-Brigg's Meanings: not, no, not (with verb — absolute prohibition), not (with modifier — negation), nothing (substantive), without (*with particle*), before (of time).

Explanation: 𐤀𐤋 negates the action of the verb that comes immediately after it. Stated another way, 𐤀𐤋 negates the action of the verb it is associated with.

Phoenician Hebrew Word: 𐤁𐤍𐤂𐤕
Transliteration: Tha-Ga-Na-Ba
1611 KJV (AV) | Gloss: thou shalt steal | you-shall-steal

Verb: 𐤁𐤍𐤂 (Ga-Na-Ba) (verb) is indexed to Strong's #1589 and means "steal".

Prefix: 𐤕 (Tha) tells us that the verb 𐤁𐤍𐤂𐤕 (Tha-Ga-Na-Ba) is written in the imperfect tense. 𐤕 also tells us that the subject of 𐤁𐤍𐤂 is the 2nd person, masculine, singular, pronoun "you", thus 𐤁𐤍𐤂𐤕 means "you will steal".

Explanation: Recall that when the negative participle 𐤀𐤋 (La-Ah) occurs before a verb, it negates the action of that verb, thus 𐤁𐤍𐤂𐤕 (Tha-Ga-Na-Ba) is means, "you will not steal".

Write your own literal translation of Exodus 20:15 in the space below:

Ancient Script: _____
_____
_____
_____

Paleo Script: _____
_____
_____
_____
_____

Exodus 20:16

| 𐤀𐤐𐤅·𐤏𐤃·𐤉𐤏𐤍𐤃·𐤕𐤏𐤍𐤄−𐤀𐤋
 false   witness   thy neighbor thou shalt beare   not

Thou shalt not beare false witnes against thy neighbour.

Phoenician Hebrew Word: 𐤀𐤋
Transliteration: La-Ah
1611 KJV (AV) | Gloss: not | not

Word: 𐤀𐤋 (negative participle) means "not" and is indexed to Strong's #3808. Brown-Driver-Brigg's Meanings: not, no, not (with verb — absolute prohibition), not (with modifier — negation), nothing (substantive), without (with particle), before (of time).

Explanation: 𐤀𐤋 negates the action of the verb that comes immediately after it. Stated another way, 𐤀𐤋 negates the action of the verb it is associated with.

Phoenician Hebrew Word: 𐤕𐤏𐤍𐤄
Transliteration: Tha-I-Na-Ha
1611 KJV (AV) | Gloss: thou shalt bear | you-shall-testify

Root Word: 𐤏𐤍𐤄 (I-Na-Ha) (verb) means to eye or (generally) to heed, i.e. Pay attention; by implication, to respond; by extension. To begin to speak; specifically to sing, shout, testify, announce -- give account, afflict (by mistake), (cause to, give) answer, bring low (by mistake), cry, hear, Leannoth, lift up, say, scholar, (give a) shout, sing (together by course), speak, testify, utter, (bear) witness" and is indexed to Strong's #6030. Brown-Driver-Brigg's Meanings: to answer, respond, testify, speak, shout; [verb form nuances:] to answer, respond to, to testify, respond as a witness, receive answer, to sing, utter tunefully.

Prefix: 𐤕 (Tha) tells us that the verb 𐤕𐤏𐤍𐤄 (Tha-I-Na-Ha) is written in the imperfect tense, "will answer". 𐤕 also tells us that the subject of 𐤏𐤍𐤄 is the 2nd person, masculine, singular, pronoun "you", thus 𐤕𐤏𐤍𐤄 means "you will answer".

Explanation: Recall that when the negative participle 𐤋𐤀 (La-Ah) occurs before a verb, it negates the action of that verb, thus 𐤕𐤏𐤍𐤄 (Tha-I-Na-Ha) is means, "you will not answer".

Phoenician Hebrew Word: 𐤁𐤓𐤏𐤊
Transliteration: Ba-Ra-I-Ka
1611 KJV (AV) | Gloss: against your neighbor | against-neighbor-of-you

Base Word: 𐤓𐤏 (Ra-I) (masculine, noun) means "an associate (more or less close) [such as] brother, companion, fellow, friend, husband, lover, neighbour, another" and is indexed to Strong's #7453. Brown-Driver-Brigg's Meanings: friend, companion, fellow, another person, fellow, fellow-citizen, another person (weaker sense).

Prefix: 𐤁 (Ba) is the preposition "in" and "with".

Suffix: 𐤊 (Ka) is the 2nd person, masculine, singular, possessive pronoun "your" and "of you", thus means "in your neighbor", "with your neighbor", "neighbor of you"

Explanation: The 𐤋𐤀 that occurred earlier in this verse is associated with the verb 𐤁𐤓𐤏𐤊, thus it negates the action of the verb 𐤁𐤓𐤏𐤊 and its meaning changes to "not in your neighbor", which is difficult to understand, so to make it easier to understand it is frequently rendered in English as "against your neighbor".

Phoenician Hebrew Word: 𐤏𐤃

Transliteration: I-Da
1611 KJV (AV) | Gloss: witness | witness-of

Word: ⊲○ (I-Da) (noun) and means "witness" and is indexed to Strong's #5707. Brown-Driver-Brigg's Meanings: witness, testimony, evidence (of things), witness (of people).

Phoenician Hebrew Word: ꟻꟿW
Transliteration: Sha-Qa-Ra
1611 KJV (AV) | Gloss: false | falsehood

Word: ꟻꟿW (Sha-Qa-Ra) (noun) means "concretely, a witness; abstractly, testimony; specifically, a recorder, i.e. Prince -- witness." and is indexed to Strong's #8267. Brown-Driver-Brigg's Meanings: lie, disappointment, falsehood, deception (what deceives or disappoints or betrays one), fraud, wrong, testify falsehood, false oath, swear falsely, falsity (of false or self-deceived prophets), in vain.

Explanation: Recall that when two nouns occur next to each other they are said to be in the construct state and we must insert the word "of" between them to render them in English. In this verse, the two nouns ꟻꟿW (Sha-Qa-Ra) and ⊲○ (I-Da) are in the construct state, thus they are often rendered in English as "false witness".

Write your own literal translation of Exodus 20:16 in the space below:

Ancient Script: _____
_____

Paleo Script: _____
_____
_____
_____

Exodus 20:17

𐤗𐤔𐤀 · 𐤃𐤌𐤇𐤗-𐤀𐤋 · 𐤏𐤓𐤉 · 𐤗𐤉𐤁 · 𐤃𐤌𐤇𐤗 · 𐤀𐤋
  wife   thou shalt couet not   thy neighbor house thou shalt couet not

𐤋𐤊 · 𐤓𐤔𐤀 𐤇𐤕 · 𐤓𐤌𐤇𐤕 · 𐤕𐤃𐤁𐤏𐤕 · 𐤏𐤓𐤉
nor any thing nor his asse no his oxe or his maid seruant nor his man seruant thy neighbor

| 𐤏𐤓𐤋 · 𐤓𐤔𐤀
thy neighbors that

Thou shalt not couet [covet] thy neighbours house, thou shalt not couet thy neighbours wife, nor his man seruant, nor his maid seruant, nor his oxe, nor his asse, nor any thing that is thy neighbours.

Phoenician Hebrew Word: 𐤀𐤋
Transliteration: La-Ah
1611 KJV (AV) | Gloss: not | not

Word: 𐤀𐤋 (negative participle) means "not" and is indexed to Strong's #3808. Brown-Driver-Brigg's Meanings: not, no, not (with verb — absolute prohibition), not (with modifier — negation), nothing (substantive), without (with particle), before (of time).

Explanation: 𐤀𐤋 negates the action of the verb that comes immediately after it. Stated another way, 𐤀𐤋 negates the action of the verb it is associated with.

Phoenician Hebrew Word: 𐤗𐤌𐤇𐤃
Transliteration: Tha-Chaa-Ma-Da
1611 KJV (AV) | Gloss: thou shalt covet | you-shall-covet

Root Word: 𐤃𐤌𐤇 (Chaa-Ma-Da) (verb) means "to delight in (beauty), greatly beloved, covet, delectable thing, (great) delight, desire, goodly, lust, (be) pleasant (thing), precious (thing)" and is indexed to Strong's #2530. Brown-Driver-Brigg's Meanings: to desire, covet, take pleasure in, delight in (verb).

Prefix: 𐤗 (Tha) tells us that the verb 𐤃𐤌𐤇 (Chaa-Ma-Da) is written in the imperfect tense, "will covet". X also tells us that the subject of ◁⩟ᗵX (Tha-Chaa-Ma-Da) is the 2ⁿᵈ person, masculine, singular, pronoun "you", thus ◁⩟ᗵX means "you will desire".

Explanation: Recall that when the negative participle ⩢ℓ (La-Ah) occurs before a verb, it negates the action of that verb, thus ◁⩟ᗵX is rendered, "you will not desire".

Phoenician Hebrew Word: X⩘⅌
Transliteration: Ba-Ya-Tha
1611 KJV (AV) | Gloss: house | house-of

Base Word: X⩘⅌ (Ba-Ya-Tha) (masculine, noun) means "court, door, dungeon, family, forth of, great as would contain, hangings," and is indexed to Strong's #1004. Brown-Driver-Brigg's Meanings: house, home, house as containing a family, household, family, dwelling habitation, human bodies (figuratively), of Sheol, of abode of light and darkness, of land of Ephraim, place, receptacle, family of descendants, descendants as organized body, inwards (metaphorically), (T*WOT*) temple, on the inside, within.

Phoenician Hebrew Word: ⩞O⩗
Transliteration: Ra-I-Ka
1611 KJV (AV) | Gloss: thy neighbor | neighbor-of-you

Base Word: O⩗ (masculine, noun) is indexed to Strong's #7453 and means "friend", "companion". Brown-Driver-Brigg's Meanings: friend, companion, fellow, another person, fellow, fellow-citizen, another person (weaker sense).

Suffix: ⩞ (Ka) is the 2ⁿᵈ person, masculine, singular, pronoun "your" or "of you", thus ⩞O⩗ means "your friend", "thy neighbor", "friend of you".

Explanation: Recall that when two nouns occur next to each other they are said to be in the construct state and the translator must insert the word "of" between them to render them in English. In this verse, the two nouns ×𐤟𐤔 (Ba-Ya-Tha) and 𐤏𐤓 (Ra-I-Ka) are in the construct state, thus when they are rendered in English 𐤏𐤓 * ×𐤟𐤔 means "house of your friend".

Phoenician Hebrew Word: 𐤀𐤋
Transliteration: La-Ah
1611 KJV (AV) | Gloss: not | not

Word: 𐤀𐤋 (negative participle) is indexed to Strong's #3808 and means "not". Brown-Driver-Brigg's Meanings: not, no, not (with verb — absolute prohibition), not (with modifier — negation), nothing (substantive), without (with particle), before (of time).

Explanation: 𐤀𐤋 negates the action of the verb that comes immediately after it. Stated another way, 𐤀𐤋 negates the action of the verb it is associated with.

Phoenician Hebrew Word: 𐤃𐤌𐤇×
Transliteration: Tha-Chaa-Ma-Da
1611 KJV (AV) | Gloss: thou shalt covet | you-shall-covet

Root Word: 𐤃𐤌𐤇 (Chaa-Ma-Da) (verb) means "to delight in -- beauty, greatly beloved, covet, delectable thing, (great) delight, desire, goodly, lust, (be) pleasant (thing), precious (thing)" and is indexed to Strong's #2530. Brown-Driver-Brigg's Meanings: to desire, covet, take pleasure in, delight in (verb).

Prefix: × (Tha) tells us that the verb 𐤃𐤌𐤇 (Chaa-Ma-Da) is written in the imperfect tense, "will covet". ✗ also tells us that the subject of ◁ℽ H (Chaa-Ma-Da) is the 2nd person, masculine, singular, pronoun "you", thus ◁ℽ H✗ means "you will covet".

Explanation: Recall that when the negative participle ⅄ℓ (La-Ah) occurs before a verb, it negates the action of that verb, thus ◁ℽ H✗ is rendered, "you will not covet".

Phoenician Hebrew Word: ✗W⅄
Transliteration: Ah-Sha-Tha
1611 KJV (AV) | Gloss: wife | wife-of

Base Word: ⱻW⅄ (Ah-Sha-Ha) (feminine, noun) means "feminine of man or mankind, woman, [wife], female" and is indexed to Strong's #802. Brown-Driver-Brigg's Meanings: woman, wife, female, woman (opposite of man), wife (woman married to a man), female (of animals), each, every (pronoun).

Explanation: ⱻW⅄ (Ah-Sha-Ha) is a feminine noun whose last pictograph is the ⱻ (Ha). ⱻW⅄ (Ah-Sha-Ha) is also in the construct state with the noun ℽO૧ that occurs immediately after it, as shown here ⱻW⅄ * ℽO૧. When a feminine noun whose last pictograph is the ⱻ (Ha) is in the construct state, the ⱻ (Ha) must be deleted and replaced by the ✗ (Tha) as shown here ~~ⱻ~~✗W⅄ (Ah-Sha-~~Ha~~-Tha) or ✗W⅄.

Phoenician Hebrew Word: ℽO૧
Transliteration: Ra-I-Ka
1611 KJV (AV) | Gloss: thy neighbor | neighbor-of-you

Base Word: ○⁹ (Ra-I) (masculine, noun) means "an associate (more or less close) [such as] brother, companion, fellow, friend, husband, lover, neighbour, another" and is indexed to Strong's #7453. Brown-Driver-Brigg's Meanings: friend, companion, fellow, another person, fellow, fellow-citizen, another person (weaker sense).

Prefix: ᗏ (Ba) is the preposition "in" and "with".

Suffix: ⴟ (Ka) is the 2nd person, masculine, singular, possessive pronoun "your" and "of you", thus ⴟ○⁹ means "in your neighbor", "with your neighbor", "neighbor of you".

Phoenician Hebrew Word: ⴟ◁ᗏ○ⴟ
Transliteration: Wa-I-Ba-Da-Wa
1611 KJV (AV) | Gloss: nor his manservant | or-male-slave-of-him

Base Word: ◁ᗏ○ (I-Ba-Da) (masculine, noun) means "servant" and is indexed to Strong's #5650. Brown-Driver-Brigg's Meanings: slave, servant, slave, servant, man-servant, subjects, servants, worshippers (of God), servant (in a special sense as prophets, Levites etc), servant (of Israel), servant (as form of address between equals).

Prefix: ⴟ (Wa) is the conjunction "and". Depending on the context, some translators render ⴟ as "or" instead of "and".

Suffix(es): ⴟ means "his" or "of him" (3rd person, masculine, singular, possessive pronoun).

Phoenician Hebrew Word: ⴟⵝⴟ𐤀ⴟ
Transliteration: Wa-Ah-Ma-Tha-Wa
1611 KJV (AV) | Gloss: nor his maidservant | or-female-slave-of-him

Base Word: ᗅᵞᗄ (Ah-Ma-Ha) (feminine, noun) is indexed to Strong's #519 and means "maid-servant". Brown-Driver-Brigg's Meanings: maid-servant, female slave, maid, handmaid, concubine.

Prefix: ᐱ (Wa) is the conjunction "and". (Depending on the context, some translators render ᐱ (Wa) as "or".

Suffix: ᐱ (Wa) is the 2ⁿᵈ person, masculine, singular, possessive pronoun "his" or "of him".

Explanation: When two nouns are in the construct state and one of them is a feminine noun whose last pictograph in the ᗅ (Ha), then the ᗅ must be deleted and replaced with the ✗ (Tha). In this case, ᗅᵞᗄ (Ah-Ma-Ha) is a feminine noun whose last pictograph is the ᗅ, therefore, the ᗅ must be deleted and replaced with the ✗ (✗ ᵞᗄ), which forms the word ✗ᵞᗄ (Ah-Ma-Tha), thus ᐱ✗ᵞᗄᐱ (Wa-Ah-Ma-Tha-Wa).

Phoenician Hebrew Word: ᐱᗅᐱᏎᐱ
Transliteration: Wa-Sha-Wa-Ra-Wa
1611 KJV (AV) | Gloss: nor his ox | or-ox-of-him

Base Word: ᐱᐱᏎ (Sha-Wa-Ra) (feminine noun) is indexed to Strong's #7794 and means "ox". Brown-Driver-Brigg's Meanings: ox, bull, a head of cattle.

Prefix: ᐱ (Wa) is the conjunction "and". (Depending on the context, some translators render ᐱ as "or".

Suffix: ᐱ (Wa) means "his" or "of him" (2ⁿᵈ person, masculine, singular, possessive pronouns).

Phoenician Hebrew Word: 𐤅𐤇𐤌𐤓𐤅
Transliteration: Wa-Chaa-Ma-Ra-Wa
1611 KJV (AV) | Gloss: nor his donkey | or-donkey-of-him

Base Word: 𐤇𐤌𐤓𐤅 (Chaa-Ma-Ra-Wa) (feminine, noun) means "a male ass, chamor from chamar, (he)ass" and is indexed to Strong's #2543. Brown-Driver-Brigg's Meanings: (he) ass.

Prefix: 𐤅 (Wa) is the conjunction "and". (Depending on the context, some translators render Wa as "or".

Suffix: 𐤅 (Wa) is the 2nd person, masculine, singular, possessive pronouns "his" or "of him", thus 𐤅𐤇𐤌𐤓𐤅 means "and his male ass), "or his male ass". The 1611 KJV (AV) renders 𐤅𐤇𐤌𐤓𐤅 as "nor his asse".

Phoenician Hebrew Word: 𐤅𐤊𐤋
Transliteration: Wa-Ka-La

1611 KJV (AV) | 𐤊𐤋 Gloss: nor anything | or-anything
Base Word: (masculine, singular, noun) means "any, all, complete, every" and is indexed to Strong's #3605. Brown-Driver-Brigg's Meanings: all, the whole, the whole of, any, each, every, anything, totality, everything.

Prefix: 𐤅 (Wa) is the conjunction "and". (Depending on the context, some translators **render** 𐤅 as "or".

Phoenician Hebrew Word: 𐤀𐤔𐤓
Transliteration: Ah-Sha-Ra
1611 KJV (AV) | Gloss: that | that

Word: 𐤀𐤔𐤓 (Ah-Sha-Ra) (genderless, numberless, relative participle) means "who, what, which, that" and is indexed to Strong's #834. Brown-Driver-Brigg's Meanings: (relative participle) which, who, that which, (conjunction) that (in object clause), when, since, as, conditional if.

Phoenician Hebrew Word: 𐤊𐤏𐤓𐤋
Transliteration: La-Ra-I-Ka
1611 KJV (AV) | Gloss: is thy neighbor's | to-neighbor-of-you

Base Word: 𐤏𐤓 (masculine, noun) means "an associate (more or less close) [such as] brother, companion, fellow, friend, husband, lover, neighbour, another" and is indexed to Strong's #7453. Brown-Driver-Brigg's Meanings: friend, companion, fellow, another person, fellow, fellow-citizen, another person (weaker sense*).*

Prefix: 𐤋 (La) is the preposition "to" or "belongs to".

Suffix: 𐤊 (Ka) is the (2nd person, masculine, singular, possessive pronoun "your" and "of you", thus 𐤊𐤏𐤓𐤋 means "to thy neighbor". "[is] thy neighbor's", "belongs to thy neighbor", "neighbor of you", "your neighbor", "to your fellow-citizen".

Write your own literal translation of Exodus 20:17 in the space below:

Ancient Script: _____
_____
_____
_____

Paleo Script: _____
_____
_____
_____

ABOUT THE AUTHOR

Dr. Yasapa MD, MBA

Dr. Yasapa's major purpose is to help the House of Yasharala to return to the Most High. Dr. Yasapa is best known for his Free Live Online Ancient Phoenician Paleo Hebrew Course. Dr. Yasapa is the founder of Zion Law School (zionlawschool.org) whose mission is to secure the blessing promised in Deuteronomy Chapter 28. Dr. Yasapa is the author of 911 Ibaryath Rescue | Ancient Phoenician Paleo Hebrew and other literature.

Made in the USA
Middletown, DE
28 March 2025

73391536R00076